A-LEVEL STUDENT GUIDE

PEARSON EDEXCEL

Economics A

Theme 4
A global perspective

Quintin Brewer

This Guide has been written specifically to support students preparing for the Pearson Edexcel A level Economics A (Theme 4) examinations. The content has been neither approved nor endorsed by Edexcel and remains the sole responsibility of the author.

Every effort has been made to trace all copyright holders, but if any have been inadvertently overlooked, the Publishers will be pleased to make the necessary arrangements at the first opportunity.

Although every effort has been made to ensure that website addresses are correct at time of going to press, Hodder Education cannot be held responsible for the content of any website mentioned in this book. It is sometimes possible to find a relocated web page by typing in the address of the home page for a website in the URL window of your browser.

Hachette UK's policy is to use papers that are natural, renewable and recyclable products and made from wood grown in well-managed forests and other controlled sources. The logging and manufacturing processes are expected to conform to the environmental regulations of the country of origin.

Orders: please contact Hachette UK Distribution, Hely Hutchinson Centre, Milton Road, Didcot, Oxfordshire, OX11 7HH. Telephone: (44) 01235 827827. Email: education@hachette.co.uk. Lines are open from 9 a.m. to 5 p.m., Monday to Friday. You can also order through our website: www.hoddereducation.co.uk.

© Quintin Brewer 2019

ISBN 978-1-5104-5807-9

First printed 2019

First published in 2019 by
Hodder Education (a trading division of Hodder & Stoughton Limited),
An Hachette UK Company
Carmelite House
50 Victoria Embankment
London EC4Y 0DZ

www.hoddereducation.co.uk

The authorised representative in the EEA is Hachette Ireland, 8 Castlecourt Centre, Dublin 15, D15 XTP3, Ireland (email: info@hbgi.ie)

Impression number 10 9 8 7 6

Year   2025

All rights reserved. Apart from any use permitted under UK copyright law, no part of this publication may be reproduced or transmitted in any form or by any means, electronic or mechanical, including photocopying and recording, or held within any information storage and retrieval system, without permission in writing from the publisher or under licence from the Copyright Licensing Agency Limited. Further details of such licences (for reprographic reproduction) may be obtained from the Copyright Licensing Agency Limited, www.cla.co.uk

Cover photo: Tomasz Zajda/Adobe Stock

Typeset by Integra Software Services Pvt. Ltd, Pondicherry, India

Printed and bound by CPI Group (UK) Ltd, Croydon, CR0 4YY

A catalogue record for this title is available from the British Library.

Contents

Getting the most from this book 4
About this book 5

Content Guidance

International economics 6
Poverty and inequality 28
Emerging and developing economies 33
The financial sector 52
The role of the state in the macroeconomy 55

Questions & Answers

Paper 2

Section A

Q1 Economic development 69
Q2 Exchange rates 70
Q3 Financial sector 71
Q4 Inequality 71
Q5 Terms of trade 72

Section B

Q6 The Gambian economy 73

Section C

Q7 Oil price increase 79
Q8 Trade war 80

Paper 3

Q1 Italy's economy 84
Q2 Robots and the economy 92

Knowledge check answers 99
Index 101

Getting the most from this book

Exam tips

Advice on key points in the text to help you learn and recall content, avoid pitfalls, and polish your exam technique in order to boost your grade.

Knowledge check

Rapid-fire questions throughout the Content Guidance section to check your understanding.

Knowledge check answers

1 Turn to the back of the book for the Knowledge check answers.

Summaries

- Each core topic is rounded off by a bullet-list summary for quick-check reference of what you need to know.

Exam-style questions

Sample student answers

Practise the questions, then look at the student answers that follow.

Commentary on the questions

Tips on what you need to do to gain full marks.

Commentary on sample student answers

Read the comments showing how many marks each answer would be awarded in the exam and exactly where marks are gained or lost.

About this book

The Pearson Edexcel A-level Economics A specification (code 9EC0) is structured into four themes and consists of three exam papers. This guide has been written to help you prepare for the papers that cover Theme 4 in the examination (9EC02 and 9EC03). The theme builds on the knowledge and skills gained in Theme 2 'The UK economy — performance and policies'. Theme 4's main emphasis is on globalisation, international trade, poverty and inequality, economic development, the financial sector and the role of the state in the macroeconomy. This theme includes material from Theme 2 — for example, aggregate demand and aggregate supply (*AD/AS*) analysis.

In this book the following areas are covered:

1 **International economics**. As an introduction to this theme, the causes of globalisation, its impacts and factors limiting globalisation are considered. This section then explores the balance of payments and exchange rates. Finally, there is an examination of the factors influencing the international competitiveness of a country's goods and services.

2 **Poverty and inequality**. In this section we consider the causes, consequences and measurement of poverty and inequality.

3 **Emerging and developing economies**. The factors influencing growth and development are examined, followed by an analysis of strategies that influence growth and development.

4 **The financial sector**. The role of financial markets, market failure in this sector and the role of central banks in the economy are considered.

5 **The role of the state in the macroeconomy**. In this section, all aspects of public finance (public expenditure, taxation, fiscal deficits and national debts) are considered. This is followed by an examination of the use of macroeconomic policies (demand-side, supply-side and direct controls) in a global context. The problems facing policymakers in applying these policies are also examined.

This guide aims to develop your macroeconomics skills in a global context, and should be used alongside the Theme 2 guide, your notes and other revision aids in the second year of study of Advanced Economics. The guide includes typical questions and answers, and explains what the examiners are looking for. Common mistakes are highlighted and several strategies for increasing your marks are suggested.

- The **Content Guidance** section provides an overview of the main topics, identifying what has to be learned and explaining the theoretical requirements of the theme.
- The **Questions & Answers** section provides questions and answers on the economic concepts and topics in Theme 4, together with explanation of the exam format and the skills that will be tested. A selection of student answers is provided to give you an idea of the level of answer required to achieve a grade A. These answers are interspersed with comments to help you understand the expectations of those who will mark your papers.

Content Guidance

■ International economics

Globalisation

The meaning of globalisation

There is no precise definition of the term 'globalisation'. It is used to refer to a variety of ways in which countries are becoming more and more closely integrated, not just in the economic sense, but also culturally and politically.

However, one of the best definitions of globalisation in the economic sense is by Peter Jay, who was the BBC's economics correspondent in 1996: 'The ability to produce any good or service anywhere in the world, using raw materials, components, capital and technology from anywhere, sell the resulting output anywhere and place the profits anywhere.'

Globalisation is not a new phenomenon because there have been many periods in history when there was considerable integration between countries, for example during the height of Roman empire. The pace of global integration increased considerably over the 50 years until the global financial crisis of 2008. However, that crisis and the more recent trend towards protectionist policies, especially by the USA, have resulted in a slowdown in this process.

Characteristics of globalisation

Globalisation, in the economic sense, is characterised by the following:
- An increase in trade as a proportion of world GDP. Figure 1 shows how world trade grew generally at a faster rate than world gross domestic product (GDP) until the financial crisis. However, between 2011 and 2016, world GDP and world trade grew at roughly the same rate.
- Increased movements of financial capital and people between countries.
- Increased international specialisation and division of labour. It is increasingly common for parts and components of products to be made in different countries and for assembly to occur in another country.
- The growing importance of global or transnational companies (TNCs).
- An increase in **foreign direct investment (FDI)**.

> **Exam tip**
>
> Globalisation is a central concept in this section so it is important that you fully understand its key features.

Foreign direct investment (FDI)
Cross-border investment by a business in one economy with the objective of obtaining a lasting interest in an enterprise resident in another economy. It may involve the acquisition by a business in one country of a business in another country.

International economics

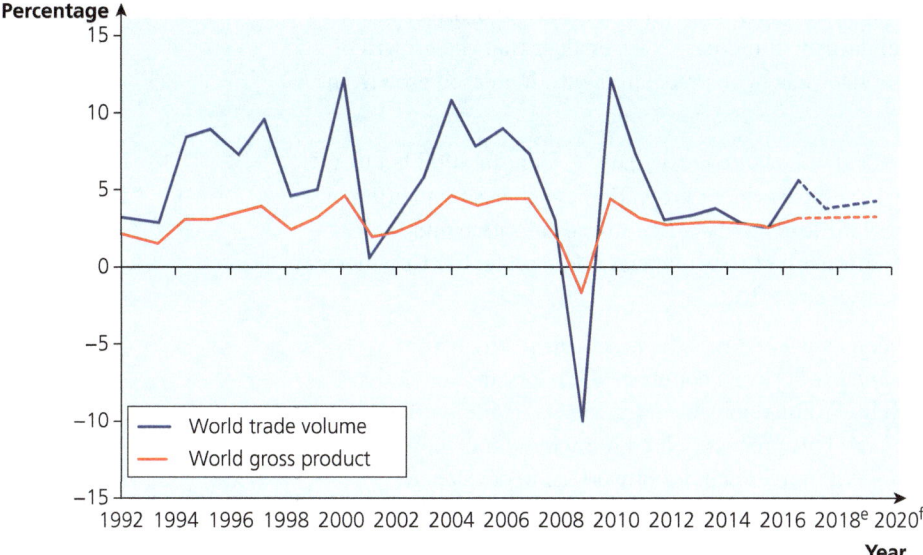

Figure 1 Growth of world trade and world GDP, 1992–2020 (e = estimates, f = forecast)
Source: UN/DESA

Factors contributing to globalisation

A variety of factors have contributed to the increased economic integration of countries.

- One of the most significant is the *fall in transport costs*. In real terms the price of transporting goods has decreased significantly, enabling goods to be imported and exported more cheaply.
- Coupled with this has been a *decline in the cost of communications*. In particular, the cost of using the internet has fallen greatly over the last 20 years and its availability has increased.
- The *lowering of trade barriers* since the Second World War has been a major factor in the growth of world trade. The World Trade Organization (WTO) — formerly the General Agreement on Tariffs and Trade — has been responsible for negotiating reductions in tariffs and other barriers to trade in rounds of talks, the most recent of which is the Doha round.
- Both the *collapse of communism* and the *opening up of China* to world trade have contributed to globalisation. Countries which were previously not open to FDI became much more integrated into the world trading system.
- *Transnational (global) companies* have taken advantage of the reduction in trade barriers and the development of the internet to organise trade on a global scale.
- *Growth in the number and size of trading blocs (regional trade agreements)* has resulted in increased trade between the member countries of these blocs. These are considered in more detail on pages 12–13.

> **Knowledge check 1**
> Identify two factors that might limit further globalisation.

Impacts of globalisation
On countries

Free trade enables the application of the *law of comparative advantage*, which suggests that, when countries specialise in the goods in which they have a comparative advantage (i.e. the goods can be produced at a lower opportunity cost), then world output and living standards will increase. It is evident that the growth of world trade in both goods and services has been associated with increased growth in real GDP.

However, the global financial crisis that became particularly evident in 2008 led to a period of *deglobalisation*, in which countries adopt protectionist policies in an attempt to protect domestic employment. This leads to a decline in specialisation and trade. Although trade recovered in the aftermath of the financial crisis, protectionist policies that restrict free trade have increased since 2016.

Further, globalisation has also been associated with *increased inequality* within some countries but *decreased inequality* between countries. One explanation is that many manufacturing and relatively unskilled jobs were transferred from developed economies to developing economies. This process helped to increase incomes in developing countries but caused a fall in real incomes of workers in developed economies. For example, since 1979, the before-tax incomes of the top 1% of America's households have increased more than seven times faster than those of the bottom 20%.

On governments
If globalisation results in an increase in economic growth and, therefore, in incomes, then governments should receive extra tax revenues. This would enable them to spend more on public services. However, **transfer pricing** by global companies may result in lower tax revenue from corporation tax.

On producers and consumers
- For producers, there are likely to be benefits in terms of lower production costs as a result of offshoring and also economies of scale.
- For consumers, globalisation may mean a wider choice of goods. Further, prices may be lower, leading to an increase in consumer surplus.

On workers
Globalisation has been criticised on the basis that it has *promoted exploitation* of workers, including the use of child labour. It is argued that globalisation has driven down wages (especially those of unskilled workers) as a share of GDP. Further, health and safety laws and regulations are usually less demanding in developing countries, which might have detrimental effects on the workforce.

On the environment
The *external costs* associated with increasing globalisation are becoming increasingly apparent, especially in relation to increased trade, air travel and environmental degradation. Global warming associated with various forms of pollution arising from increased trade is one example of external costs arising from increased globalisation.

Specialisation and trade
Absolute and comparative advantage
This law states that, even if one country has an **absolute advantage** in the production of all goods, it can still benefit from specialisation and trade if it

Transfer pricing
This occurs when a global company manages its accounting of internal transactions within the company to show the highest profits in the country in which corporation tax is lowest.

Knowledge check 2
Why might globalisation increase inequality in a developed economy?

Exam tip
The effects of globalisation overlap with many other areas of this theme, so it is useful to revisit these once you have understood those topics.

Absolute advantage
This means that a country can produce more of a product than another country.

International economics

specialises in the production of goods in which it has a **comparative advantage** (i.e. if it specialises in the production of those products in which its opportunity cost is lowest). The crucial requirement is that there must be a difference in the opportunity cost of producing the products.

Assumptions underlying the theory of comparative advantage

- no transport costs
- no trade barriers
- constant returns to scale, i.e. average cost of production is constant
- perfect mobility of resources between different uses
- buyers/consumers have perfect knowledge

The following example illustrates the theory of comparative advantage:

Suppose countries A and B both produce two products — palm oil and televisions. They can both produce the following amounts of these products with the same quantity of resources:

Country	Palm oil	Televisions
A	20,000	10,000
B	8,000	8,000

Clearly, country A has an absolute advantage in the production of both palm oil and televisions. If each country devotes half its resources to the production of each product, then output would be as follows:

Country	Palm oil	Televisions
A	10,000	5,000
B	4,000	4,000
Total	14,000	9,000

To determine whether trade will be worthwhile, the *opportunity costs* must be calculated:

	Opportunity cost of producing 1 kilogram of palm oil	Opportunity cost of producing 1 television
A	½	2
B	1	1

From the table, it can be seen that country A has a comparative advantage in palm oil (because the opportunity cost is lower than in country B), while country B has a comparative advantage in televisions.

For trade to be beneficial, the terms of trade must lie between the opportunity cost ratios. In this case, the terms of trade must lie between 1 kilogram of palm oil and 2 kilograms of palm oil for one television.

The terms of trade are measured as follows:

$$\frac{\text{index of export prices}}{\text{index of import prices}} \times 100$$

You should note that, if the opportunity costs were the same, then there would be no benefit from specialisation and trade.

> **Comparative advantage** This means that a country can produce a product at a lower opportunity cost than another country, meaning that it has a relative advantage in producing that product.

> **Exam tip**
>
> It is useful to learn a numerical example to illustrate comparative advantage for use in an examination.

Content Guidance

Limitations of the principle of comparative advantage
- Transport costs might outweigh the benefits of comparative advantage.
- Similarly, trade barriers might distort comparative advantage.
- Increased specialisation and production might result in rising average costs caused by diseconomies of scale.

However, despite these limitations, many economists support the view that free trade brings net benefits to the global economy.

Advantages and disadvantages of specialisation and trade
Advantages
- Efficient resource allocation: specialisation and free trade based on comparative advantage result in an efficient allocation of resources.
- Higher world output and, therefore, higher living standards.
- Lower prices and more choice for consumers.
- Incentive for domestic producers to become more efficient.
- Larger markets for firms, enabling them to benefit from economies of scale.

Disadvantages
- The law of comparative advantage is based on unrealistic assumptions (see above).
- For developing economies, specialisation in the production of primary products might prevent diversification into more productive manufacturing industries.
- There is a danger of overdependence on imports, especially those of strategic importance.
- A country's goods and services may be uncompetitive, resulting in a persistent trade deficit.

> **Knowledge check 3**
> Identify two possible benefits of free trade to consumers.

Patterns of trade
Factors influencing the pattern of trade
The pattern of world trade changes over time, as shown in Figure 2. It may be explained by a range of factors, including the following:
- *Changes in comparative advantage.* Comparative advantage may change as a result of factors such as changes in labour skills and productivity, discovery of new natural resources, the adoption of new technology and improvements in infrastructure.
- *Emerging and developing economies.* The pattern of world trade has also been greatly affected by the growth of emerging and developing economies, for example China, which is now a major manufacturer. Figure 2 shows how exports from developing economies as a proportion of total world exports increased from about 31% in 2000 to about 42% in 2016. It also shows a significant growth of trade between developing countries (south–south trade) from 11% in 2001 to 21.4% in 2016.
- *Trading blocs and bilateral trading agreements.* Since the Second World War there has been a significant growth in the number and size of **trading blocs**. Given that most of these have free trade between member countries and that customs unions have common external tariffs, trading blocs have had an important influence on the pattern of world trade. Similarly, bilateral trade agreements (agreements between

> **Trading bloc** A group of countries that trade freely but protect themselves from imports from non-members.

International economics

two countries) have also affected trade patterns. One recently formed trading bloc is the Comprehensive and Progressive Agreement for Trans-Pacific Partnership (CPTPP), which came into force in December 2018. It will eliminate 95% of tariffs on goods trade between 11 countries around the Pacific rim, including Australia, Canada, Japan, Malaysia and Vietnam.

- *Changes in relative exchange rates.* A long-term change in a country's exchange rate against those of other countries will affect the relative competitiveness of that country's goods and services and so will influence trading patterns. For example, if country A's currency depreciates against those of other countries, then its goods and services will become more competitive and so its exports are likely to increase and imports decrease relative to those of other countries.

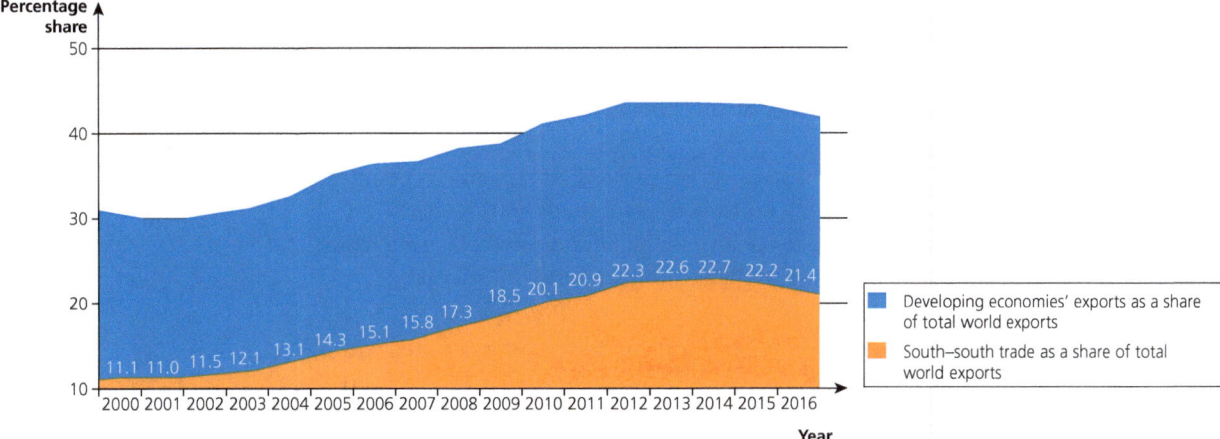

Figure 2 Share of developing economies in world exports, 2000–2016

Source: WTO World Trade Statistical Review 2018

Terms of trade

Calculation of the terms of trade

The **terms of trade** (T/T) are calculated by using the following formula:

$$\text{T/T} = \frac{\text{index of export prices}}{\text{index of import prices}} \times 100$$

Therefore, the terms of trade is the relationship between the price of exports and the price of imports or the rate at which exports exchange for imports.

Terms of trade The average price of a country's exports relative to the average price of its imports.

Factors influencing a country's terms of trade

The following are examples of some of the factors which can influence a country's terms of trade.

- *Relative inflation rates.* If the UK inflation rate is higher than that of its trading partners then export prices will be rising relative to import prices, so causing a rise in the UK's terms of trade.
- *Changes in raw material prices.* For a developed country which imports most of its raw materials, a rise in imported raw material prices would cause a fall in its terms of trade.

Theme 4 A global perspective

Content Guidance

- *Changes in exchange rates*. If a country's exchange rate increases relative to those of other countries then its export prices would rise and its import prices would fall, so causing its terms of trade to increase.
- *Tariffs*. If a country imposes a tariff on imported goods then this would cause an increase in import prices and so would result in a fall in the country's terms of trade.
- *Dependency on primary products*. If a country is dependent on primary products then, according to the *Prebisch–Singer hypothesis*, it may find that its terms of trade decrease over time (see pages 35–36).

Impact of changes in a country's terms of trade

- *On living standards*. An upward movement in the terms of trade is usually referred to as an 'improvement' because it implies that the country has to export less to gain a given quantity of imports. This implies a higher standard of living for the citizens of that country. In contrast, a fall in the terms of trade is referred to as a 'deterioration' because it implies that more must be exported to gain a given quantity of imports.
- *On the balance of payments on current account*. An upward movement in a country's terms of trade would decrease the competitiveness of its goods and services because its export prices would be rising relative to its import prices. Consequently, the country's balance of payments on current account are likely to deteriorate. (see page 16).
- *On the rate of inflation*. A fall in a country's terms of trade may be associated with a higher rate of inflation if the fall was caused by an increase in the price of imported raw materials.
- *On developing countries*. Resource-rich developing countries sometimes suffer from what is called the 'resource curse'. This arises because ownership of minerals and fuels causes an appreciation in the exchange rates of the currencies of these countries and, in turn, an increase in the terms of trade. However, this results in a loss of competitiveness of their manufactured goods and services, leading to slower economic growth than might otherwise have been the case.

Knowledge check 4
What factors could cause an increase in a country's terms of trade?

Trading blocs and the World Trade Organization (WTO)
Types of trading blocs
Regional trade blocs are intergovernmental associations that manage and promote trade activities for specific regions of the world. Trading blocs may take several forms:
- *Free trade areas*. Trade barriers are removed between member countries, but individual members can still impose tariffs and quotas on countries outside the area. An example is the North Atlantic Free Trade Area (NAFTA).
- *Customs unions*. The characteristics of customs unions include free trade between member states and a *common external tariff* on goods imported from outside the bloc. Examples include the European Union (EU) and the Customs Union of Russia, Belarus and Kazakhstan (formed in 2010).
- *Common markets*. These are customs unions but with the added dimension that it is not only goods and services that can be moved freely within the area (between member states), but also factors of production (especially labour). Examples include Mercosur and the East African Common Market.

Exam tip
Trading blocs are not blocks on trade such as tariffs. They are groups of countries that agree to trade freely between themselves.

- *Monetary unions.* These are customs unions that adopt a *common currency*. The eurozone area of the EU is an example of such a union.

Costs and benefits of regional trade agreements

Costs

- *Trade diversion.* Trade may be diverted away from low-cost producers outside the bloc to high-cost producers within the bloc because of the existence of tariffs on goods from outside the bloc.
- *Distortion of comparative advantage.* The existence of trade restrictions on goods from countries outside the agreement will distort comparative advantage and lead to a less efficient allocation of resources, lowering global economic growth.
- *Loss of independent monetary policy.* This would be relevant to countries in monetary unions which would be unable to control their own interest rates and exchange rates.

Benefits

- *Trade creation.* The removal of trade barriers between member countries of the bloc will result in increased specialisation and trade between them.
- *Increase in FDI.* Global companies may wish to invest inside a trading bloc to avoid trade restrictions.

In addition, monetary unions may enjoy further benefits, including the following:

- *Elimination of transactions costs.* In other words, there would be no costs involved in changing currencies when goods are imported or exported.
- *Price transparency.* A single currency means that consumers have the ability to compare prices more easily across national borders.
- *Elimination of currency fluctuations between member countries.* This eliminates uncertainty and might help to attract FDI.

Role of the WTO in trade liberalisation

Essentially, the WTO performs two key functions:

- to promote free trade among the 164 member countries through so-called 'rounds of talks'
- to settle trade disputes between members

Possible conflicts between regional trade agreements and the WTO

The existence of trading blocs has two significant consequences, as described above:

- trade creation
- trade diversion

While trade creation is a goal of the WTO, the trade diversion which results from regional trade agreements clearly is not.

Nevertheless, it may be argued that the growth in both the number and size of regional trade agreements has contributed to the WTO goal of promoting free trade.

Knowledge check 5

What is the key feature of any regional trade agreement (trading bloc)?

Content Guidance

Restrictions on free trade

Reasons for restrictions on free trade

The term 'protectionism' refers to measures designed to limit free trade. Arguments supporting the need for protectionism include the following:

- *To protect infant industries.* This argument might be particularly relevant to developing countries that are in the process of industrialisation. Without protection, infant industries might be unable to compete because they have yet to establish themselves and are too small to benefit from economies of scale.
- *To protect geriatric industries.* These are industries that might demand protection so that they have time to restructure and rationalise production, which would enable them to become competitive once again. Typically, these occur in developed economies that are losing their comparative advantage.
- *To ensure employment protection.* Cheap imports might threaten jobs in the domestic economy and workers might demand that the government takes action to limit imports.
- *To prevent dumping.* 'Dumping' refers to goods exported to another country at below the average cost of production. It is a form of predatory pricing and, if it can be proved, is illegal under the WTO rules. This is one of the few arguments in favour of protectionism that can be justified in terms of economic theory because it unfairly distorts comparative advantage.
- *To correct a balance of payments deficit on current account.* Restrictions on imports might help to reduce the imbalance between the value of imports and the value of exports. However, under a system of floating exchange rates, it is possible that this correction will happen automatically.
- *To restrict imports from countries whose health and safety regulations and environmental regulations are less stringent.* Some argue that developing countries might have an unfair competitive advantage because production is not subject to the same laws and regulations that apply to developed countries, so enabling them to produce at a lower average cost.
- *For strategic reasons.* A country might introduce protectionist policies on goods of strategic importance in time of war so that it is not dependent on imports. Food, defence equipment and energy are items frequently used as examples of such goods.
- *To raise tax revenue.* Tariffs might be an important source of tax revenue for developing countries.
- *In retaliation.* Barriers to trade might be imposed by a country because another country has restricted the import of its goods.

Types of restrictions on trade

There are numerous ways in which free trade can be prevented. The most common are *tariffs*, *quotas*, *subsidies to domestic producers* and *non-tariff barriers*. In countries where the exchange rate is not freely floating, the authorities might also hold down the value of the currency artificially to give their goods a competitive advantage.

Tariffs

These are sometimes referred to as customs duties: they are simply taxes on imported goods. Figure 3 illustrates the effect of a tariff.

International economics

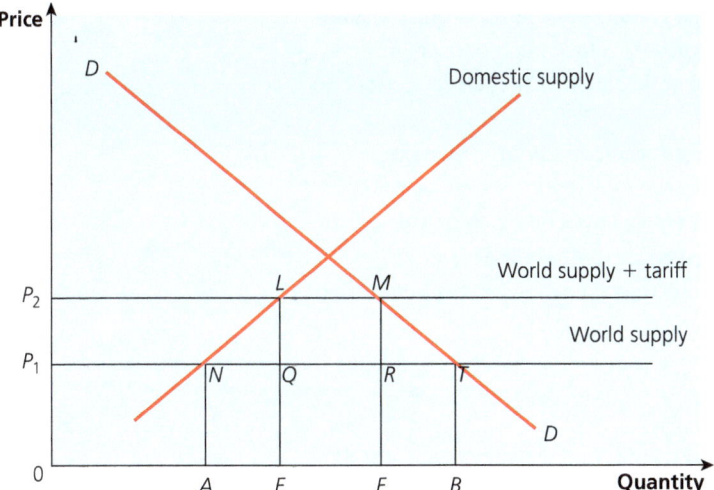

Figure 3 The effects of imposing a tariff

Before the tariff is imposed:
- the price paid by consumers is OP_1
- domestic output is OA and domestic demand is OB
- imports are AB

Once the tariff is imposed:
- the price paid by consumers rises to P_2, so reducing consumer surplus by P_1P_2MT
- domestic output rises to OE, so increasing producer surplus by P_1P_2LN
- imports fall to EF
- tax revenue to the government is $QLMR$
- net welfare loss areas are NLQ and RMT

Quotas

Import quotas place a physical restriction on the amount of goods that can be imported. They have similar effects to those of tariffs, in that the price of imported goods will rise and domestic producers should gain more business. However, unlike tariffs, the government does not receive any revenue.

Subsidies to domestic producers

Grants given to domestic producers artificially lower their production costs, making their goods more competitive. Subsidies therefore act as a barrier to trade.

Non-tariff barriers

These take a variety of forms, including labelling, health and safety regulations, environmental standards and documentation in country of origin. In effect, such regulations increase the costs of foreign producers and so act as a barrier to trade.

Impact of protectionist policies

- *On consumers.* Higher prices and less choice.
- *On producers.* Less incentive for domestic producers to become more efficient.

> **Exam tip**
> Knowledge of the tariff diagram is very useful in explaining a range of possible effects.

> **Knowledge check 6**
> How do tariffs affect comparative advantage?

Content Guidance

- *On governments.* A government would receive tax revenue from tariffs but subsidies to domestic producers would incur a cost on taxpayers. Once such barriers are introduced, it might prove difficult to remove them because of the adverse effect on domestic producers.
- *On living standards.* Protectionism results in a less efficient resource allocation because trade barriers distort comparative advantage and reduce specialisation, which will result in lower world output and, therefore, lower living standards.
- *On equality.* Trade barriers imposed by developed countries on goods from developing economies could increase inequality between these two sets of countries.

Balance of payments

The components of the balance of payments

The balance of payments is a record of all financial transactions between one country and other countries. When there is an inflow of foreign currency into the UK, this is recorded as a positive item, whereas when there is an outflow of foreign currency, this is recorded as a negative item.

The main components of the balance of payments are the *current account* and the *capital and financial account*.

The current account

This is composed of the following:
- *The trade balance.* This is the value of goods and services exported minus the value of goods and services imported. The trade balance may be separated into the *trade in goods balance* and the *trade in services balance*.
- *The income balance (now renamed primary income).* This is income flows into the country from non-residents minus income flows out of the country from residents to non-residents. Income refers to compensation to employees and investment income, for example.
- *Current transfers (now renamed secondary income).* This relates to workers' remittances, donations, tax payments, foreign aid and grants.

The capital and financial account

This comprises transactions associated with changes of ownership of the UK's foreign financial assets and liabilities. A key factor influencing the financial account is FDI. Also included are portfolio investment in shares and bonds, changes in foreign exchange reserves and the short-term capital flows, often referred to as 'hot money' flows, associated with speculation.

The balance on this account should exactly offset the current account balance (although, in practice, there is a significant component comprising errors and omissions).

Causes of deficits and surpluses on the current account

Causes of current account deficits

These include:
- low productivity relative to other countries, meaning that the country's goods and services are not competitive internationally

International economics

- a high inflation rate relative to other countries
- an overvalued exchange rate
- dependence on highly priced imported raw materials
- relocation of manufacturing industries to low-wage countries
- protectionism by other countries
- poor quality goods relative to those produced by other countries

Causes of current account surpluses

These include:
- relatively high productivity, meaning that the country's goods and services are more internationally competitive
- relatively low inflation rate
- undervalued exchange rate
- abundance of minerals, fuels and agricultural produce which is in high demand by other countries
- protectionist policies designed to reduce imports

The UK's current account

For many years, the UK has had a deficit on the current account. In particular, the trade in goods balance has deteriorated over a number of years, as shown in Figure 4.

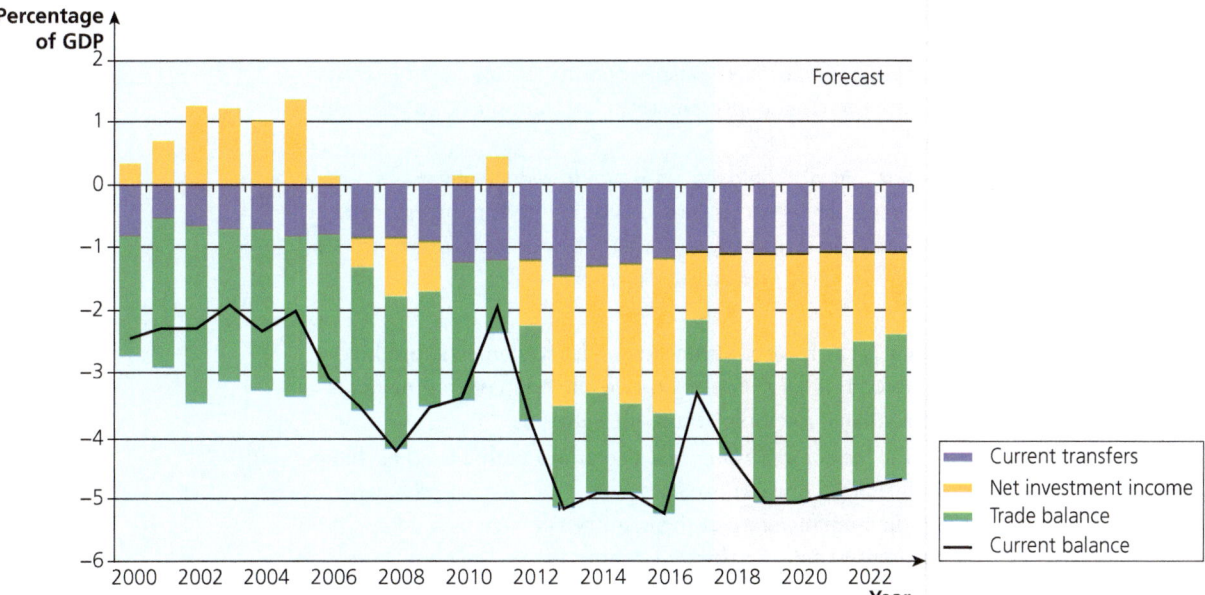

Figure 4 The UK balance of payments on current account as a percentage of GDP
Source: Office for Budget Responsibility, *Economic and fiscal outlook*, March 2019

The main reasons for the UK's current account deficit include:
- the high value of sterling 1996–2008
- continuous economic growth 1992–2008 — the UK has a high marginal propensity to import and so rising real incomes have led to a significant increase in imports

- relatively low productivity (particularly since the financial crisis) resulting in higher average costs
- the relocation of manufacturing to countries with lower labour costs (e.g. China and eastern European countries)
- slow growth in the eurozone resulting in weak demand for the UK's exports
- the deterioration in 'net income balance', i.e. net income from interest, profits and dividends
- increased protectionism by the USA

> **Knowledge check 7**
> What factors might cause a balance of trade deficit?

Measures to reduce a country's imbalance on the current account

Possible measures to reduce a *current account deficit* include the following:
- *Supply-side policies designed to increase productivity and competition.* These would help to improve the competitiveness of the country's goods and services and so lead to an increase in exports and a decrease in imports. These may be *market-based*, e.g. privatisation, deregulation and contracting out of public services, or *interventionist*, e.g.:
  - education and training aimed at increasing the productivity of the workforce
  - investment in infrastructure
  - investment allowances and tax breaks to stimulate the purchase of capital equipment
- *Expenditure-reducing policies.* These could include deflationary fiscal policy, i.e. measures to reduce aggregate demand by raising taxes and/or decreasing government expenditure. If direct taxes were raised then disposable income would fall, causing a fall in consumption and, consequently, a fall in imports, so resulting in an improvement in the balance of trade.

  Deflationary monetary policy may also be used. This would reduce aggregate demand by raising interest rates. However, it should be noted that many countries have independent central banks so it is not within their governments' power to raise interest rates as a means of reducing a current account deficit.
- Expenditure-switching policies. These include:
  - *protectionist policies* such as tariffs, quotas and subsidies to domestic producers. However, it should be noted that WTO rules and membership of trading blocs might make it impossible/illegal to employ these measures.
  - *devaluation/depreciation of the country's currency.* A country with a fixed exchange rate could devalue its currency. However, under a system of floating exchange rates, a depreciation of the exchange rate of the country's currency could only be engineered by reducing interest rates or through quantitative easing but these monetary tools would not be available to a government if the central bank is independent. A detailed analysis of the effects of a depreciation/devaluation of the exchange rate of a country's currency is considered on pages 22–23.

> **Knowledge check 8**
> What is the distinction between expenditure-switching and expenditure-reducing policies?

Significance of global trade imbalances

Like the UK, the USA has experienced large current account deficits, while, in contrast, China and Germany have experienced huge current account surpluses. Whether such global imbalances can be sustained in the long run is a major question. On the one hand, if the deficits are easily financed by inflows on the financial account, there may be no cause for concern. Further, under a system of floating exchange rates, over time, there should be an automatic adjustment (i.e. a deficit would cause the exchange rate to fall). On the other hand, continuous deficits by the USA have, in effect, been financed by the Chinese, which may not be a sustainable option in the long run.

Exchange rates

The *nominal exchange rate* is the number of units of the domestic currency that can purchase a unit of a given foreign currency.

The *real exchange rate* is calculated to measure the movements of the competitiveness of the country's currency in relation to another country's currency on the basis of inflation differential between the countries. In other words, the real exchange rate is the nominal exchange rate adjusted to reflect the different inflation rates in the countries of the two currencies concerned.

Effective exchange rates are estimated to measure the movements of a country's currency value or average exchange rate in a basket of currencies of trade-partner countries.

A country's *trade-weighted exchange rate* is a common form of the effective exchange rate. It is the average exchange rate in a basket of currencies, weighted by the amount of trade with each country.

Exchange rate systems

The exchange rate is the rate at which one currency exchanges for another. In other words it is the *price* of one currency in terms of another, e.g. £1 = $1.50. There are three main exchange rate systems: floating, fixed and managed.

Floating exchange rates

Under a system of floating exchange rates, market forces (supply of, and demand for, the currency in the foreign exchange market) determine the value at which one currency exchanges for another.

Fixed exchange rates

Under a system of fixed exchange rates, the value at which one currency exchanges for another is fixed by the central bank or the government against another currency or basket of currencies or gold.

Managed exchange rates

Under a system of managed exchange rates, market forces determine the value at which one currency exchanges for another but intervention by the central bank influences the exchange rate of the currency.

Distinction between revaluation and appreciation of a currency

A *revaluation* of a currency only occurs under a system of fixed exchange rates when the government decides to increase the value of its currency against other currencies or gold.

Appreciation of a currency occurs under a system of floating exchange rates when the value of a currency increases against another currency as a result of the operation of market forces.

Content Guidance

Distinction between devaluation and depreciation of a currency

A *devaluation* of a currency only occurs under a system of fixed exchange rates when the government decides to decrease the value of its currency against other currencies or gold.

Depreciation of a currency occurs under a system of floating exchange rates when the value of a currency decreases against another currency as a result of the operation of market forces.

Factors influencing floating exchange rates

Factors influencing the value of a currency					
Relative inflation rates	Relative interest rates	The state of the economy	The balance of payments on current account	Political factors	Speculation

Figure 5 Factors influencing the exchange rate of a country's currency

As Figure 5 shows, a variety of factors can influence the value of a country's currency against other currencies, including the following:

- *Relative inflation rates.* If the country's inflation rate is higher than that of its major competitors then, according to *purchasing power parity (PPP) analysis*, it would be expected that the value of the currency would fall. The PPP rate is the rate at which a particular product would be sold at the same price in the UK and abroad when expressed in a common currency.
- *Relative interest rates.* If the UK has higher interest rates than those of other countries, then foreigners with surplus balances are likely to place them in UK banks. This would increase the demand for sterling and cause the value of the pound to increase against other currencies.
- *The state of the economy.* If, for example, the UK economy is performing well, this will increase the confidence of speculators and foreign investors, who will buy sterling, so causing its value to rise against other currencies.
- *The balance of payments on current account.* If there is a persistent deficit on the current account, then the supply of the currency would be high relative to demand for it and the value of the currency would be expected to fall. In practice, this factor is not significant because the flows of money associated with trade are small compared with 'hot money' flows and other transactions recorded in the financial account.
- *Political stability.* In developing countries, instability may cause a loss of confidence in the country's currency.
- *Speculation.* The exchange rate might be affected by speculation concerning a range of possible events, including factors such as the future state of the economy, a change in government or impending strikes.

Knowledge check 9

How might an increase in the rate of inflation in Venezuela affect its exchange rate relative to the US dollar?

International economics

Government intervention in currency markets

There are two main ways by which the exchange rate of a currency against other currencies may be influenced: foreign currency transactions and interest rates.

Foreign currency transactions

The central bank can intervene in the foreign exchange market in attempts to influence the exchange rate of its currency against other currencies.

To bring about an appreciation in the exchange rate of the currency against other currencies, the central bank would buy its currency on the foreign exchange market in exchange for foreign currency. The increase in demand for the domestic currency would cause an increase in the value of its currency against foreign currencies.

In contrast, to engineer a depreciation of the exchange rate of its currency, the central bank would sell its own country's currency on the foreign exchange market in exchange for foreign currency. This increase in supply would cause a fall in the value of the currency against foreign currencies.

Use of interest rates

To bring about an appreciation of the currency against other currencies, the central bank would raise interest rates. For example, between May 2018 and July 2019 Pakistan's central bank raised the base rate of interest from 6.5% to 13.25%. One aim of this was to make its currency, the rupee, more attractive for foreign citizens to place money in Pakistan's banks, so increasing demand for rupees on the foreign exchange market.

A reduction in interest rates would have the opposite effect, making it less attractive for citizens and foreign nationals to hold money in that country's banks. This would cause an increase in supply of the currency on the foreign exchange market and so reduce its value against other currencies. The same effect might result from quantitative easing (see Theme 2) which has the effect of increasing the money supply.

Competitive devaluation/depreciation

The meaning of competitive devaluations/depreciations

Competitive devaluations or depreciations are sometimes referred to as **currency wars** because a devaluation/depreciation by one country results in other countries taking measures to devalue/depreciate their currencies.

The effects of competitive devaluations/depreciations

These could cause:
- an increase in the rate of inflation because imports would become more expensive
- a decline in world trade because of the uncertainties associated with fluctuating exchange rates

Further, countries could retaliate by imposing protectionist measures, e.g. tariffs, as happened in the 1930s.

Currency war When a country deliberately reduces the value of its currency in order to gain a competitive advantage and this results in other countries taking similar action.

Content Guidance

Effects of a change in the exchange rate of a currency

On the current account of the balance of payments

A depreciation/devaluation makes a country's goods and services more competitive and so should lead to an improvement in its current account.

Suppose that the value of the pound against the dollar falls, e.g. from £1 = $2.00 to £1 = $1.50. There are two effects.

- It will make the price of goods exported from the UK *decrease* in the country of sale (e.g. a bottle of UK whisky costing £20 would have sold for $40 in the USA but will now sell for $30).
- It will make the price of goods imported into the UK *increase* (e.g. a $10 bottle of Californian wine would have been priced at £5 in the UK but will now cost £6.67).

Therefore, a fall in the value of the pound makes UK goods more competitive. The consequence of this is that demand for exports is likely to rise while demand for imports is likely to fall. This is likely to cause a reduction in the size of the deficit on the current account of the balance of payments. However, this depends on the price elasticities of demand for imports and exports — see next section.

The Marshall–Lerner condition

For there to be an improvement in the current account, the Marshall–Lerner condition must be fulfilled — i.e. the sum of the price elasticities of demand (PEDs) for imports and exports must be greater than 1.

The J-curve effect

It is possible that there could be a time lag before the full effects of the depreciation of the currency work through the economy, such that the sum of the price elasticities of demand would be between 0 and 1 in the short run but greater than 1 in the long run. This gives rise to the *J-curve effect*, as illustrated in Figure 6.

Initially, the current account deteriorates, since demand for imports is price inelastic because of contracts or stocks of goods. Also, demand for exports may be inelastic because it takes time for consumers to adjust to the price changes. In the longer term, demand for both imports and exports may become more elastic and, if the Marshall–Lerner condition is fulfilled, the current account will improve.

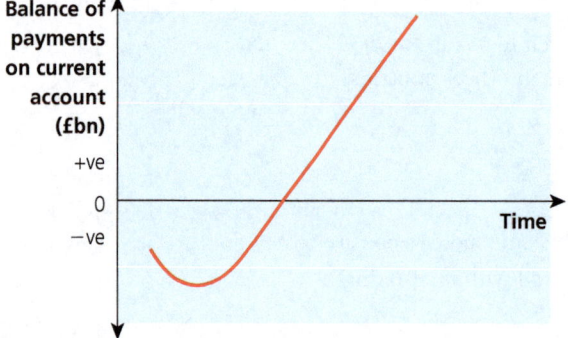

Figure 6 The J-curve effect

> **Exam tip**
>
> Remember that a fall in the value of a country's currency causes an increase in the price competitiveness of its goods and services, whereas a rise causes a decrease in the price competitiveness of that country's goods and services.

> **Knowledge check 10**
>
> What would be the effect on the current account of the balance of payments following a depreciation in the value of the currency if the sum of PEDs for exports and imports is between 0 and 1?

International economics

On economic growth and employment/unemployment

If there is an increase in net exports following a depreciation in the value of a country's currency against other currencies, then aggregate demand (AD) will increase, causing an increase in real output. In turn this should result in an increase in employment and a decrease in unemployment.

On the rate of inflation

Following a depreciation, inflationary pressures could arise from two sources:
- the increase in AD, described above, resulting from a rise in net exports
- imported inflation: the rise in import prices, especially of raw materials and commodities, is likely to increase costs of production, causing a leftward shift in the aggregate supply curve and so to an increase in the rate of inflation

On foreign direct investment (FDI) flows

A depreciation in the exchange rate of country A's currency against others would potentially make it more attractive for foreign companies to invest in that country because a unit of a foreign currency would buy more units of country A's currency.

However, if the depreciation is indicative of a lack of confidence in the country's economy, then FDI inflows may not increase.

International competitiveness

A country's 'international competitiveness' refers to its ability to sell its goods and services in domestic and international markets at a price and quality that is attractive in those markets. Competitiveness may be measured in terms of *price* or *non-price factors*. The non-price factors include quality, design, reliability and availability.

Measures of international competitiveness

Relative unit labour costs

This refers to the measurement of labour costs in one country relative to those in another country. To make international comparisons, the figures are converted into a single currency and expressed as an index number.

Relative export prices

These might be affected by factors such as productivity (relative to other countries). This may be measured in terms of labour productivity, which is output per worker per hour worked.

The global competitiveness index

This is a composite measure devised by the World Economic Forum and is based on factors such as infrastructure, macroeconomic stability, health and education, degree of efficiency in the labour and goods market, technological readiness and innovation.

Exam tip

Remember to include both price and non-price factors in discussions of international competitiveness.

Content Guidance

The top 10 rankings for 2018 were:

1. USA
2. Singapore
3. Germany
4. Switzerland
5. Japan
6. Netherlands
7. Hong Kong SAR
8. UK
9. Sweden
10. Denmark

The least competitive economies were Haiti, Yemen and Chad.

Factors influencing international competitiveness

Real exchange rate

Competitiveness is determined by a variety of factors but one of the most important is a country's **real exchange rate**, which is the nominal exchange rate adjusted for changes in price levels between economies. More precisely:

$$\text{real exchange rate} = \text{nominal exchange rate} \times \frac{\text{domestic price level}}{\text{foreign price level}}$$

There will be a depreciation in the real exchange rate if the nominal exchange rate falls or if the prices of goods abroad rise relative to prices in the home country. Therefore, a fall in the real exchange rate will cause an increase in the competitiveness of a country's goods.

In contrast, the real exchange rate will increase if the nominal exchange rate rises or if the UK price level rises relative to the foreign price level. Consequently, an appreciation of the real exchange rate is associated with a fall in the country's competitiveness.

Wage costs and non-wage costs

Wage costs are the most important cost of production for many industries. Consequently, if wages are higher in the UK than in China, it is likely that the prices of the goods in the UK will be higher than those of China. However, the relationship between labour productivity and wages is crucial in influencing unit labour costs.

Non-wage costs are also significant for international competitiveness. These include:

- national insurance contributions paid by employers (taxes on employment)
- health and safety regulations
- environmental regulations
- employment protection and anti-discrimination laws
- contributions into company pension schemes

These non-wage costs are frequently much higher in developed countries than in developing countries and so have the effect of reducing the international competitiveness of goods and services from developed countries.

> **Real exchange rate**
> The nominal exchange rate adjusted to reflect different inflation rates (and, therefore, purchasing power) of the currencies concerned.

International economics

Other factors

Governments can try to improve international competitiveness through a variety of *supply-side policies*. Of particular relevance are the following:
- *education and training schemes* which may increase the occupational mobility of labour. Education and training influence the level of *human capital*, which is defined as the knowledge and skills of the workforce
- *public sector reform* aimed at reducing red tape and regulations
- government expenditure to improve *infrastructure* (e.g. roads, railways, telecommunications, power generating stations and water supply)
- *privatisation and deregulation*
- incentives for *investment* such as tax breaks if companies use profits for investment or for research and redevelopment
- measures to increase *labour market flexibility* such as making it easier to hire and fire workers, reducing the strength of trade unions and allowing the use of flexible hours contracts

It should be noted that international agreements are likely to prevent individual countries increasing their competitiveness by raising tariffs. For example, the UK cannot simply introduce tariffs on goods from other EU countries because of its legal obligations as a member of the EU. Similarly, most countries are members of the WTO, whose rules prevent a country unilaterally imposing protectionist measures unless there is justifiable case.

Further, it is not possible for the UK government to devalue its currency because the pound is a floating currency. Also, since the Bank of England is independent, the government cannot directly engineer a depreciation in the exchange rate of the pound through a reduction in interest rates because control over interest rates is not in its hands.

The significance of international competitiveness

Benefits of being internationally competitive

A country can enjoy several advantages of being internationally competitive, including:
- a surplus on its balance of trade
- export-led growth leading to an increase in real incomes
- low levels of unemployment
- an increase in FDI

Problems of being internationally uncompetitive

A fall in international competitiveness is likely to be reflected in a deterioration in the balance of trade. In turn, this could result in an increase in unemployment, especially in industries in which exports are significant. A fall in exports could have a negative multiplier effect on GDP, so causing a reduction in economic growth.

> **Exam tip**
>
> Refer back to what you learned in Theme 2 about supply-side policies and look out for new measures being introduced by governments.

> **Knowledge check 11**
>
> What would happen to international competitiveness if a country's productivity increased at a slower rate than that of its major competitors?

Examination skills and concepts
- Understanding of the growing interdependence between economies.
- Ability to differentiate between the costs and benefits of globalisation.
- Ability to explain the basis of free trade in terms of the law of comparative advantage.

Content Guidance

- Ability to use the tariff diagram to illustrate the implications of tariffs, including welfare losses.
- Evaluation of the possible conflicts between trading blocs and the WTO.
- Understanding the main components of the balance of payments accounts and being able to assess the impact on these components of changes in external factors (e.g. an increase in FDI).
- Ability to analyse the effect of changes in the exchange rate on other macroeconomic variables.
- Assessing the case for and against membership of the eurozone.
- Understanding different measures of competitiveness.
- Understanding the real exchange rate.
- Ability to evaluate the significance of competitiveness for an economy.
- Ability to evaluate different measures to increase competitiveness.

Common examination errors

- Confusion between absolute and comparative advantage.
- Imprecise diagrammatic analysis, especially in the case of tariffs.
- Misinterpreting trading blocs as protectionist measures.
- Confusion between a balance of payments deficit on current account and a fiscal deficit.
- Confusion over the difference between components of the current account and components of the financial account.
- A lack of clarity in explaining the effects of a change in the exchange rate on the current account of the balance of payments and on the pattern of trade.
- Assuming that countries and groups such as the USA, EU and UK can 'devalue' or 'revalue' their currencies.
- Confusion between production and productivity.
- Confusion between the nominal and real exchange rate.

Links and common themes

- Application of opportunity cost (Theme 1) to the law of comparative advantage.
- Supply and demand analysis in considering tariffs and quotas (Theme 1).
- The balance of payments accounts (Theme 2).
- Causes of changes in exchange rates under a system of floating exchange rates: application of supply and demand analysis (Theme 1).
- Price elasticities of demand for imports and exports (Theme 1) when considering exchange rate changes.
- This section has close links with productivity, supply-side policies and the balance of payments (Theme 2).
- There are links with other parts of this theme, including the factors influencing growth in developing countries.

International economics

Summary

- Globalisation refers to the increased economic integration between countries through, for example, increased trade.
- Factors contributing to increased globalisation include: the lowering of trade barriers; lower communication and transport costs; the opening up of China.
- Benefits of globalisation may be analysed using the law of comparative advantage.
- The law of comparative advantage states that trade between two nations can be beneficial to both if each specialises in the production of a good with lower opportunity cost.
- The WTO's key roles are to promote free trade and settle trade disputes.
- Trading blocs are groups of countries that trade freely among themselves but set trade barriers against non-members.
- Arguments for protectionism include: employment protection; prevention of dumping; protection of infant industries; retaliation.
- Protectionism may take several forms, such as tariffs, quotas, subsidies to domestic producers and non-tariff barriers.
- The current account of the balance of payments is mainly concerned with the trade in goods and services between countries.
- The financial account is important when considering FDI and 'hot money' flows between countries.
- Current account deficits may be caused by factors including: a lack of competitiveness; an overvalued exchange rate; relatively low productivity; and non-price factors such as poor quality and design.
- Global imbalances arise when some countries have persistent current account deficits while others have persistent current account surpluses.
- In a free market, exchange rates are determined by the supply of and demand for currencies on the foreign exchange market.
- However, exchange rates may be fixed in relation to another currency or managed by the central bank intervening in the foreign exchange market.
- A floating exchange rate may be affected by confidence; relative interest rates; relative inflation rates; expectations about the future state of the economy.
- Revaluation or appreciation of a currency implies that its exchange rate has increased against other currencies.
- Devaluation or depreciation of a currency implies that its exchange rate has decreased against other currencies.
- A change in the exchange rate of a country's currency will affect a country's current account of the balance of payments, economic growth, unemployment, the rate of inflation and FDI.
- International competitiveness reflects the ability of a country to sell its goods and services in world markets.
- The key factors influencing competitiveness are: relative unit labour costs; relative productivity rates; non-wage factors including national insurance contributions; regulations; non-price factors such as quality, design and reliability.
- International competitiveness could be increased by supply-side policies or by a depreciation of the country's currency.

Content Guidance

■ Poverty and inequality

Absolute and relative poverty

Absolute poverty

According to the World Bank, people are considered to be living in absolute poverty if their incomes fall below the minimum level to meet basic needs such as food, shelter, clothing, access to clean water, sanitation facilities, education and information. This minimum level is usually called the *poverty line*.

In 2015, 10% of the world's population lived on less than US$1.90 a day, down from nearly 36% in 1990. Although poverty rates have declined in all regions, progress has been uneven:

- Two regions, East Asia and Pacific (47 million extreme poor) and Europe and Central Asia (7 million) have reduced extreme poverty to below 3%.
- More than half of the extreme poor live in sub-Saharan Africa. It is likely that if that continues, by 2030 nearly 9 out of 10 extreme poor will be in sub-Saharan Africa.
- The majority of the global poor live in rural areas, are poorly educated, employed in the agricultural sector, and under 18 years of age.

One of the UN sustainable development goals is to 'End poverty in all its forms everywhere'.

Relative poverty

People are considered to be in relative poverty if they are living below a certain income threshold in a particular country. This may vary from country to country. Therefore, the concept of relative poverty is:

- subjective
- subject to change over time
- not comparable between countries (i.e. someone deemed relatively poor in the USA would be regarded as being incredibly rich in Malawi)

Relative poverty arises from inequality (see below).

Measures of absolute and relative poverty

Measure of absolute poverty

Absolute poverty is based on a set standard that is consistent over time and between countries, referring to the ability of individuals or groups to meet their basic needs.

The World Bank defines absolute poverty as the percentage of the population of a country living on less than $1.90 a day (PPP) at constant 2011 prices.

> **Exam tip**
>
> All countries will have some people living in relative poverty because incomes are unevenly distributed. However, it is possible for a country to have no one living in absolute poverty because this is defined in terms of an internationally agreed measure.

Poverty and inequality

Measure of relative poverty

Relative poverty is measured in comparison with other people in the country. Therefore, there will always be some people who are relatively poor in any given country. Relative poverty lines are defined in relation to the overall distribution of income or consumption in a country, so if a person is living below a certain income threshold in a particular country they would be classified as being in relative poverty. For example, in the EU, people whose income is less than 60% of median income are considered to be 'at risk of poverty' and are said to be relatively poor.

> **Knowledge check 12**
> Will relative poverty ever be eliminated?

Causes of changes in absolute and relative poverty

Changes in any of the following factors may result in changes in absolute and relative poverty:

- economic growth
- education and training
- social benefits (transfer payments)
- taxes
- wage rates and national minimum wages
- ownership of assets and their prices, e.g. houses and shares

In addition, changes in the following might have a significant impact in developing countries:

- aid
- debt relief
- fair-trade schemes
- property rights

Inequality

Distinction between wealth and income inequality

Wealth is a *stock* concept. Wealth inequality refers to inequality based on value of tangible assets, e.g. property, shares, works of art.

Income, on the other hand, is a *flow* concept. Income inequality refers to inequality based on incomes from wages, rent and profit.

Measurements of income inequality: the Lorenz curve and the Gini coefficient

The Lorenz curve

The degree of inequality can be measured using a Lorenz curve, which plots the cumulative percentage of the population against the cumulative percentage of total income. The 45° line represents perfect equality such that the poorest 10% of the population would receive 10% of the income, the poorest 20% of the population would receive 20% of the income and so on. The curved line represents an unequal distribution of income. In Figure 7, the areas *A* and *B* are used in the calculation of the Gini coefficient (see below).

Content Guidance

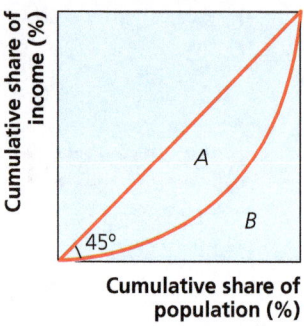

Figure 7 The Lorenz curve

The Gini coefficient

This is a measure of the degree of inequality in a country. It is calculated as follows:

$$G = \frac{A}{A + B}$$

where A represents the area between the diagonal line and the Lorenz curve and B represents the area under the Lorenz curve. The Gini coefficient will have a value of between 0 and 1, with 0 representing absolute equality (i.e. the Lorenz curve and line of total equality are merged) and 1 absolute inequality (i.e. the Lorenz curve would lie along the horizontal and vertical axes). The Gini coefficient may also be expressed as a percentage:

$$G = \frac{A}{A + B} \times 100$$

Causes of income and wealth inequality within countries

Inequality may be the result of a variety of factors, including:
- education and training
- wage rates
- unemployment
- social benefits (transfer payments)
- progressive and regressive taxes
- inheritance
- ownership of assets and their prices, e.g. houses and shares
- pensions (state and private)

Causes of income and wealth inequality between countries

Inequality between countries depends on a variety of factors including:
- differences in natural resources
- geography, e.g. whether or not a country is land-locked or close to large markets
- differences in governance: for example, it is sometimes argued that centrally planned economies are less efficient at allocating resources than those that have an element of market forces in allocating resources

Knowledge check 13

What would happen to the Lorenz curve if inequality increased within a country?

Exam tip

Make sure that you can draw an accurately labelled Lorenz curve diagram and can show an increase or decrease in inequality.

Poverty and inequality

- political instability; civil wars
- natural disasters
- population growth and structure

Impact of economic change and development on inequality

According to Simon Kuznets, inequality is an inevitable cost associated with economic development because owners of resources will become wealthier as opportunities for profitable investment increase. In contrast, the movement of workers from the countryside to towns keeps wages down. As a result inequality increases in the early stages of industrialisation. After a certain level of industrialisation, inequality will decrease as the welfare state develops.

It may also be argued that inequality itself is a constraint on economic change and development for the following reasons:

- the very poor will have no collateral and so will be unable to start their own businesses
- absolute poverty could remain high in countries where inequality is high
- those on low incomes will have a low marginal propensity to save, so limiting funds available for investment, while those on high incomes may spend a large amount of their incomes on imported goods or may transfer their incomes to other countries (known as *capital flight*: see pages 37–38)

Further, there may be socially undesirable consequences of inequality, such as an increase in the crime rate, which might have an adverse effect on growth and development.

Significance of capitalism for inequality

The free market economy and capitalism were considered in Theme 1 where inequality was identified as one of the consequences of such an economic system. The reason relates back to two key features of the free market economy:

- private ownership of resources
- the profit motive

It is inevitable that private ownership of resources will enable those who accumulate more assets to be richer relative to those who own few resources. The profit motive is necessary in a capitalist, free market economy to encourage entrepreneurs to take the risks involved in production. Such entrepreneurs are likely to become much richer than workers if their businesses prove to be successful.

Examination skills and concepts

- Understanding the difference between absolute poverty and relative poverty.
- Understanding of how absolute and relative poverty may be measured.
- Ability to explain the factors influencing income and wealth inequality.
- Understanding of the Lorenz curve and of the Gini coefficient.

Content Guidance

Common examination errors
- Confusion between absolute and relative poverty.
- Confusion between income and wealth.
- Imprecision in drawing a Lorenz curve diagram.
- Failing to interpret the Lorenz curve and Gini coefficient correctly.

Links and common themes
- This section has links with the next section on emerging and developing countries, especially the factors influencing growth and development.

Summary
- Absolute poverty refers to people who have insufficient resources to meet their basic needs, whereas relative poverty refers to those living below a certain income level.
- Wealth and income inequality may be caused by a variety of factors, including: inheritance; ownership of assets; education; wage rates; age; pension entitlements; unemployment; taxes, and social benefits.
- Inequality may be measured by reference to the Lorenz curve and Gini coefficient.
- Inequality may limit growth and development, e.g. because those in absolute poverty will be unable to obtain loans to start businesses.

Emerging and developing economies

Measures of development

The human development index (HDI)

The HDI is a composite index of development and includes three elements:
- education (the mean years of schooling for an adult aged 25 and expected years of schooling for a pre-school child)
- health (life expectancy at birth)
- real GNI per head at purchasing power parities

This index results in a number between 0 and 1: the higher the value, the higher the level of development.

The inequality-adjusted HDI (IHDI)

The IHDI is published alongside the HDI and takes into account how human development is distributed. Countries that are very unequal see their human development scores fall more than those that are less unequal. Therefore, the difference between the HDI and the IHDI represents the 'loss' in potential human development due to inequality.

The multi-dimensional poverty index (MPI)

The global MPI is composed of ten indicators corresponding to the same three components as the HDI: education, health and standard of living. Multi-dimensional poverty is made up of several factors that constitute poor people's experience of deprivation — such as poor health, lack of education, inadequate living standard, disempowerment, poor quality of work and the threat of violence.

Therefore, the global MPI combines two aspects of poverty:
- incidence, i.e. the percentage of people who are poor
- the intensity of people's poverty, i.e. the average of the components identified above in which poor people are deprived

Other indicators

These include:
- the proportion of the male population engaged in agriculture
- energy consumption per person
- the proportion of the population with access to clean water
- mobile phones per thousand of population
- the proportion of the population with internet access

Content Guidance

Factors influencing growth and development

While all countries face constraints on their growth and development (Figure 8), there is an enormous difference in the scale of the constraints affecting developed and developing countries. It is important, therefore, to have some knowledge of specific countries in order to give relevant examples.

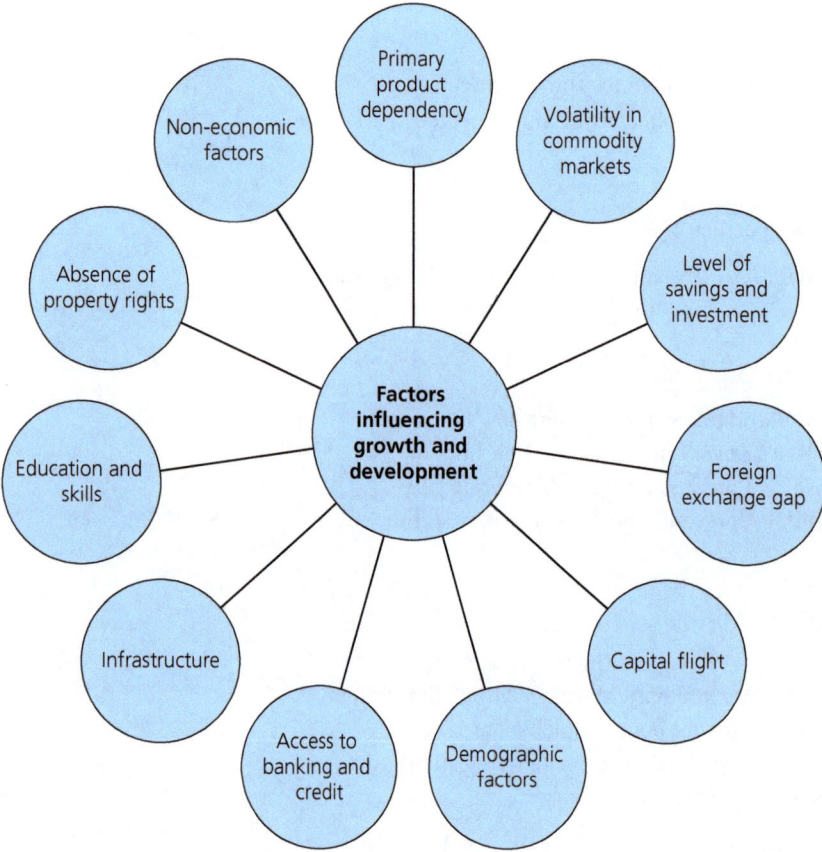

Figure 8 Factors influencing growth and development

Primary product dependency

Primary products may be divided into hard commodities, such as copper, tin and iron ore, and soft commodities, which include most agricultural crops, such as wheat, palm oil, rice and fruit. A range of issues face countries dependent on primary products, including the following:

- *Price fluctuations.* See next section.
- *Fluctuations in export earnings.* Given that demand for many primary products is price inelastic, a sharp fall in the price of a commodity could result in a significant fall in export earnings. In turn, this would lead to a deterioration in the country's trade balance.
- *Fluctuations in tax revenues.* A fall in the price of a primary product would cause a fall in the revenues of producers. In turn, this could result in a reduction in tax revenues from profits made by producers.

Emerging and developing economies

- *Difficulty of planning investment and output.* Price fluctuations cause uncertainty, which is a deterrent to investment.
- *Natural disasters.* Extreme weather such as hurricanes, tornadoes, droughts and tsunamis can cause severe disruption to the production of primary products, especially agricultural products.
- *Protectionism by developed countries.* For example, the huge subsidies given to US cotton farmers have created great difficulties for Indian cotton farmers, who are unable to compete; the EU's Common Agricultural Policy has meant that there is no free access to European markets for food from developing countries.
- *Low income elasticity of demand for primary products.* The Prebisch–Singer hypothesis states that the terms of trade between primary products and manufactured goods tend to deteriorate over time.
- *Dutch disease.* A country well endowed with a natural resource (in high global demand) may face an appreciation in its exchange rate which would reduce the competitiveness of its other goods and services.

The Prebisch–Singer hypothesis

This theory suggests that countries that export commodities would be able to import less and less for a given level of exports. Prebisch and Singer examined data over a long period of time and found that the terms of trade for primary commodity exporters *did* have a tendency to decline. A common explanation for this is that the income elasticity of demand for manufactured goods is greater than that for primary products, especially food. Therefore, as incomes rise, the demand for manufactured goods increases more rapidly than demand for primary products. Consequently, the prices of manufactured goods rise relative to the prices of primary products, so causing a decline in the terms of trade for countries dependent on the export of primary products.

The theory may be criticised on the following grounds.
- First, some countries have developed on the basis of their primary products (e.g. Botswana: diamonds).
- Second, if a developing country has a comparative advantage in a primary product, then its resources will be used more efficiently by specialising in the production of that product.
- Third, primary product prices rose sharply until the middle of 2008 while the prices of many manufactured products were falling.

Some economists argue that, in the case of food, prices are likely to increase as world population grows and incomes in countries such as China and India rise, so causing higher demand for many foods traditionally eaten by those in developed countries.

Similarly, the outlook for countries such as Bolivia is good. Nearly half the world's known reserves of lithium (which can be used to make batteries for hybrid and electric vehicles) are located in Bolivia. Given environmental concerns and regulations the demand for electric cars and, therefore, the demand for lithium can be expected to rise sharply in the future.

Knowledge check 14
Why is the price of many commodities unstable?

Content Guidance

In contrast, countries producing and exporting copper, such as Chile, were faced with a 50% fall in price between the middle of 2011 and 2016. In the following three years there was some recovery in the price.

Volatility in commodity markets

Demand for, and supply of, commodities tend to be price inelastic. In the case of demand, this is because they are required in the production of other goods for which demand is also price inelastic, such as pasta, bread and steel. Supply is inelastic because a long growing period is required for soft commodities (most agricultural commodities) while for hard commodities, e.g. coal and diamonds, considerable time is required for developing new mines. Consequently, any demand-side or supply-side shock will result in a significant price change. In turn, price changes will result in fluctuations in producers' incomes and foreign exchange earnings. For example, since demand is price inelastic, then a fall in price will cause total revenue to fall and, therefore, the foreign currency earnings from exports to fall.

Any shift in the supply curve or the demand curve would cause a sharp change in price. A shift in the supply curve of an agricultural commodity might occur if there is a drought, while an earthquake might disrupt the production of copper mining. Since demand is price inelastic, then a leftward shift in the supply curve would cause a significant increase in price.

Figure 9 shows the effect on the price of wheat of both a leftward shift in the supply curve from S_1 to S_2, e.g. caused by a drought, and a rightward shift in the supply curve from S_1 to S_3, e.g. caused by a bumper harvest.

> **Exam tip**
>
> Always be prepared to include some theoretical models in your analysis. Evaluation is then possible by reference to real examples.

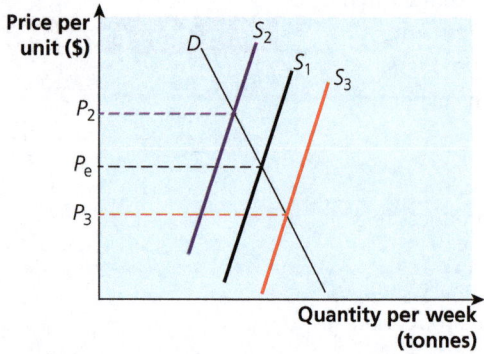

Figure 9 The effect of a change in conditions of supply on the price of wheat

The diagram shows that shifts in the supply curve would cause a significant price rise when there is a decrease in supply and a significant price fall when there is an increase in supply.

Similarly, a change in the conditions of demand would cause a significant price change because supply is price inelastic. Demand for many commodities has increased for a number of reasons, including:

- an increase in world population, which is now over 7 billion
- an increase in real incomes, which has led to increased demand for many commodities (for example, the demand for beef, which requires large amounts of grain for animal feed, has increased significantly)
- an increased demand for grain to be used for fuel

Emerging and developing economies

Levels of savings and investment

Many developing countries a have low GDP per capita and consequently they hold inadequate savings to finance the investment seen as essential to achieve economic growth and development. The Harrod–Domar model, shown in Figure 10, illustrates the problem.

> **Knowledge check 15**
>
> Identify two criticisms of the Harrod–Domar model.

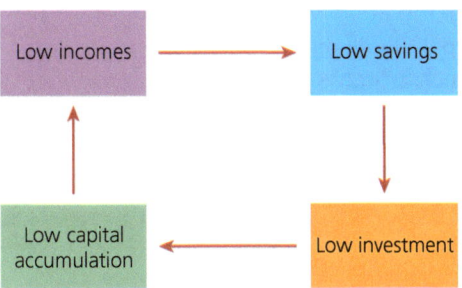

Figure 10 The Harrod–Domar model

Foreign exchange gap

Associated with the savings gap, many developing countries face a shortage of foreign exchange. This may be the result of a variety of factors, including:

- dependence on export earnings from primary products
- dependence on imports of capital goods and other manufactured goods
- capital flight (see next section)
- debt

Debt is a particular problem for some emerging and developing countries and has become an issue for some developed countries, for example Greece, since the financial crisis. Many developing countries borrowed money at times of low interest rates, only to find that they were struggling to service the debt (pay the interest on it) some years later. Debt has become a problem for variety of reasons, including:

- risky decisions to borrow money to finance major investment projects at times when the world economy was strong and/or the prices of the goods which they were exporting were high
- an increase in oil prices, which presented particular problems over the periods of such price increases
- a fall in the value of the currencies of developing countries, which increased the burden of foreign debt
- loans taken out to finance expenditure on military equipment

When considering debt, it is important to remember that the absolute size of the debt is less important than a country's ability to finance it. This may be measured by examining data on debt service payments as a percentage of GDP or debt service payments as a percentage of export earnings.

Capital flight

This occurs when individuals or companies decide to remove deposits in domestic banks and place them in foreign banks or buy shares or other assets in foreign countries. This has serious implications, for example:

Theme 4 A global perspective

- it contributes to the savings gap and foreign currency gap, and consequently:
  - it restricts economic growth
  - it reduces the tax base because the country loses any tax payable on these assets

Demographic factors

Population growth is particularly rapid in some of the poorest countries of the world, such as Nigeria, whose population increased from 42.8 million in 2000 to 200 million in 2019. Meanwhile, population is falling in some developed countries, such as Italy and Germany.

Population growth may be analysed in relation to the views of Thomas Malthus, who predicted at the end of the eighteenth century that famine was inevitable because population grows in geometric progression, whereas food production grows in the form of an arithmetic progression. His predictions were proved to be incorrect for Britain in the nineteenth century because of significant improvements in agricultural productivity. However, some economists believe that Malthus's view is still relevant for some of the poorest developing countries. In these countries the growth of the population is greater than the growth in GDP, with the result that GDP per capita is falling. This has been the case in Nigeria between 2014 and 2018.

Access to credit and banking

Inability to borrow money is obviously important both for entrepreneurs who wish to start up new businesses and for existing firms that may need credit to fund the purchase of capital and raw materials. In some developing economies, banking services are poor or almost non-existent. However, *microfinance schemes* have helped to provide extremely poor families with small loans (microcredit) to help them engage in productive activities or grow their tiny businesses. In particular, they can help the poor to increase income, build businesses and reduce vulnerability to external shocks. Further, the growth of mobile banking in countries such as Kenya has resulted in an increase in the proportion of Kenyans with access to a financial account from 42% in 2011 to 75% in 2018.

For more information on microfinance schemes, see page 42.

Infrastructure

Infrastructure covers the whole range of structures that are essential for an economy to operate smoothly. Infrastructure includes:
- transport
- telecommunications
- energy supply
- water supply
- waste disposal

Poor infrastructure will make it difficult to attract both domestic and foreign investment and thus presents a significant obstacle to growth and development. On the other hand, a country rich in a natural resource demanded by other countries might benefit from FDI: a transnational company might provide some infrastructure to the country in order to facilitate its business investment, e.g. new roads, thus benefiting the whole country.

Exam tip

Capital flight and interest payments on debt result in an outflow of foreign currency from the current account of the balance of payments, thus making it more difficult for developing countries to finance imports.

Knowledge check 16

What will happen to a country's dependency ratio if the birth rate remains high but the death rate decreases?

Education and skills

A country whose education standards are poor and where there is a low school enrolment ratio is likely to experience a slow rate of economic growth because the productivity of the workforce will be low. It will also act as a deterrent to transnational companies to invest in the country because of the costs involved in educating and training workers.

Absence of property rights

If individuals do not have property (ownership) rights, e.g. over land or property, then this might act as a constraint on economic growth and development. The reason is that, without any form of collateral, they would find it difficult to secure a bank loan which they might require to start a business.

Non-economic factors

Corruption, poor governance, wars and political instability

Corruption is usually defined as the use of power for personal gain. Corruption acts as a constraint on development when it causes an inefficient allocation of resources.

Poor governance implies that the rulers of a country have adopted policies that result in the country's resources being allocated inefficiently. Corruption may also mean that the country is poorly governed and that resources are not allocated efficiently. In addition, intervention by the government in the economy might result in a net welfare loss (government failure — see Theme 1).

Civil wars, such as those that have occurred in Syria, Sudan and the Democratic Republic of the Congo, disrupt growth and development. Indeed, in so far as they actually cause destruction of infrastructure and the death of many people, they might negate any progress made in previous years.

Similarly, *political instability* results in a considerable degree of uncertainty, which does not provide a sound basis in which businesses can operate.

All the above issues can deter both domestic investment and FDI and so limit the possibilities for growth and development.

Further, geography may have a significant impact on a country's ability to develop. For example, economic development is limited in a land-locked country such as Niger because of isolation from world markets resulting from high transportation costs.

> **Knowledge check 17**
> Why might an absence of property rights restrict growth and development?

> **Exam tip**
> It is useful to have case study examples to include in your answers to illustrate these constraints on growth and development. Study at least one country from South America, Asia and Africa.

Strategies influencing growth and development

A range of strategies may be used to promote growth and development but there is no one simple prescription: each country is individual, having a different history, geography and natural resources. Consequently, policies that may appear to have worked in one country will not be successful in another country. In practice, it is likely that a combination of strategies may be required, with the particular blend being dependent on the characteristics and needs of that country. Various strategies are outlined below. As with the previous section, the emphasis is on developing countries but some of these strategies may also be relevant to developed economies. Figure 11 summarises these strategies.

Content Guidance

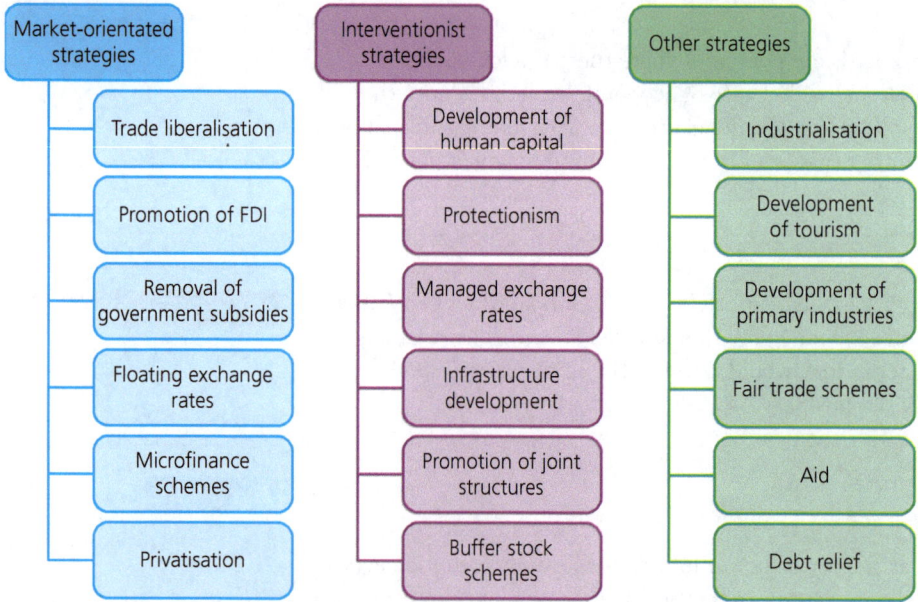

Figure 11 Strategies influencing growth and development

Market-orientated strategies

These strategies work through the operation of market forces. They usually involve measures to remove government intervention.

Trade liberalisation

Trade liberalisation refers to the lowering or complete removal of trade barriers such as tariffs, quotas and non-tariff barriers. Countries that have had sustained growth and prosperity have opened up their markets to trade and investment. By liberalising trade and focusing production on industries in which the country has a comparative advantage, economic growth should increase.

The effect of a reduction in tariffs on a particular country is illustrated in Figure 12.

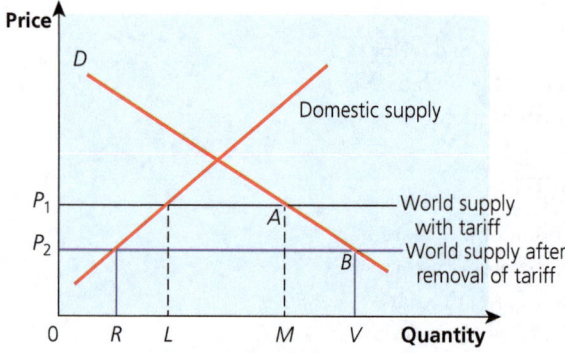

Figure 12 Effect of a reduction in tariffs

When tariffs are reduced, the price falls from P_1 to P_2, resulting in an increase in consumer surplus of P_2P_1AB. Imports will increase from LM to RV.

Emerging and developing economies

The benefits of trade liberalisation include the following:
- *Consumers* benefit because liberalised trade can help to lower prices and, therefore, increase consumer surplus. The choice and quality of goods and services available will also increase.
- *Companies* may benefit because liberalised trade diversifies risks and enables firms to benefit from economies of scale resulting in lower long-run average costs.
- A *country's economy* may benefit from trade liberalisation because it promotes competition, and usually leads to increased investment and productivity.

The OECD has estimated that if G20 economies reduced trade barriers by 50%, then there would be:
- *increased employment*: for example, a 0.3–3.3% rise in jobs for lower-skilled workers and a 0.9–3.9% rise for higher-skilled workers, depending on the country
- *higher real wages*: an increase in real wages of 1.8–8% for lower-skilled workers and 0.8–8.1% for higher-skilled workers, depending on the country
- *increased exports*: all G20 countries would see a boost in exports. In the long run, many G20 countries could see their exports rise by 20% and in the eurozone by more than 10%

On the other hand, trade liberalisation may have drawbacks including the following:
- Some domestic industries may be unable to compete with competition from foreign suppliers. This could result in a loss of jobs in these industries.
- It might have adverse effects on the environment because there would be an increase in the external costs associated with trade.
- Infant industries in developing and emerging economies may not be able to survive competition from companies in established overseas countries.

Knowledge check 18
Why might trade liberalisation limit development in a developing economy?

Exam tip
Trade liberalisation implies the removal of trade barriers and you should be able to assess the advantages and disadvantages of such policies for developing countries.

Promotion of foreign direct investment (FDI)

FDI is viewed as being desirable because it acts as an injection into the circular flow, provides employment opportunities, and increases the productive potential of the economy. Therefore, governments may try to promote FDI in a variety of ways, including:
- Reduction in corporation tax — the tax on company profits.
- Increases in tax incentives and grants towards investment.
- Increasing the ease of doing business in a country. The World Bank produces an annual report that ranks countries on the ease of doing business. It presents quantitative indicators on business regulations and the protection of property rights.
- Liberalisation of labour laws, e.g. ease of hiring and firing workers; zero hours contracts.
- Reducing trade barriers so that it is easier to import components and to export finished goods.

Removal of government subsidies

Subsidies distort the operation of market forces and are likely to result in a misallocation of resources. Governments in India, Egypt and Indonesia have been trying to cut food and energy subsidies because of their cost and the distorting effects that they have on their economies.

Content Guidance

Floating exchange rates

Allowing the exchange rate of a currency to float might result in a depreciation against other currencies, so making the country's goods and services more competitive. This might encourage global companies to invest in that country since the currency is no longer overvalued.

Microfinance schemes

Microfinance, as we have seen (page 38), is a means of providing extremely poor families with small loans (microcredit) to help them engage in productive activities or grow their tiny businesses. It can help the poor to increase income, build businesses and reduce vulnerability to external shocks. The pioneer of microfinance was Muhammad Yunus, who established the Grameen Bank in Bangladesh.

The key features of microfinance schemes are as follows:
- microcredit insists on repayment (in contrast to development aid)
- interest is charged to cover the costs involved
- the focus is on groups whose alternative sources of finance are limited to the informal sector, where the interest charged would be high

The main clients of microfinance are:
- women (who make up more than 97% of the clients)
- the self-employed, often household-based entrepreneurs
- small farmers in rural areas
- small shopkeepers, street vendors and service providers in urban areas

Despite some obvious successes, microfinance has been criticised on several grounds:
- concerns have been raised about the repayment rates, collection methods and questionable accounting practices
- on a larger scale, some argue that an overemphasis on microfinance to combat poverty will lead to a reduction of other assistance to the poor, such as official development assistance or aid from non-governmental organisations (NGOs)

Privatisation

The sale of publicly owned assets to the private sector through the issue of shares has been a popular policy in developed economies for many years and has also been adopted by some developing countries. Privatisation is seen as a way of increasing efficiency and productivity as a result of competition and the profit motive, which are characteristics of the private sector.

Interventionist strategies

These strategies involve intervention by the state in order to influence the allocation of resources. Various forms of intervention are considered below.

Development of human capital

Countries with poor education standards and low school enrolment ratios are likely to experience slow rates of economic growth. Therefore, improvements in access to education and in the quality of education would help to increase the skills and productivity of the workforce. Such improvements would also encourage FDI by global companies in these countries.

Protectionism

This strategy is aimed at constructing a path towards diversification and industrialisation. Its characteristics include placing controls on imported goods, e.g. tariffs and quotas. This helps to promote *import substitution* (i.e. replacement of imports with domestically produced manufactured goods). It is sometimes referred to as an *inward-looking strategy*.

The aim of protectionism is to enable a country to diversify in a controlled way until it has built a strong domestic base. This approach will be most effective where a country's domestic market is large enough to enable industries to benefit from economies of scale. Once achieved, industry will be strong enough to cope with foreign competition.

However, there are some drawbacks to this approach:
- *comparative advantage* is distorted and so resources will not be allocated efficiently
- the *lack of competition* could result in inefficiency

Managed exchange rates

Some countries try to maintain overvalued exchange rates with the aim of keeping down the cost of imports, especially of oil, raw materials and capital equipment. In turn, this would make it easier for them to grow and develop.

Infrastructure development

Infrastructure refers to the physical and organisational structures and facilities, such as buildings, roads, railways, power supplies and the internet, needed for the operation of a society or enterprise. Without these it would be difficult for a country to grow and develop. A striking example of such infrastructure development is China's Belt and Road Initiative (BRI). It is aimed at improving China's links with the rest of the world. It is intended to close the development gap between wealthy Beijing and China's eastern states, and the underdeveloped west of China. The idea is to promote development along five corridors out of China: land routes through central Asia to Europe; to the Middle East and Southeast Asia; and sea routes connecting Chinese ports to Europe and to the South Pacific.

Promotion of joint ventures

A joint venture is an association of two or more businesses for the purpose of engaging in a specific enterprise for profit. Firms might enter into joint ventures to combine strengths and increase their competitive advantage while minimising risks.

Examples:
- Jaguar Land Rover has a joint venture with Chinese company Chery Automobile for the purpose of manufacturing and distributing luxury cars to Chinese consumers.
- Kellogg Company entered into a joint venture agreement with Wilmar International Limited for the purpose of selling and distributing cereal and snack foods to consumers in China.
- In 2017 Renault and Nissan Alliance announced a joint venture with the Dongfeng Motor Group, a Chinese car maker, to produce electric cars.

Content Guidance

Buffer stock schemes

One method of reducing price instability is to adopt schemes which involve storing and releasing the commodity in times of surplus and shortage. The following analysis describes one way by which a **buffer stock scheme** might operate.

- A ceiling price: this is the maximum price that would be allowed.
- A floor price: this is the minimum price that would be allowed.
- A buffer stock would be established: this could be operated either by a government or by a producers' association. It would store or release stocks as required in order to reduce price fluctuations to the agreed limits.

Figure 13 illustrates the operation of a buffer stock scheme:

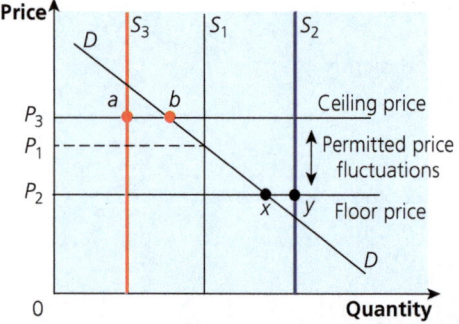

Figure 13 The operation of a buffer stock scheme

- In year 1, the equilibrium price is P_1 so no action is required because the price is within the permitted price range.
- Suppose supply is S_2 in year 2, then, to prevent the price from falling below the floor price, xy would be removed from the market and stored in a buffer stock.
- If supply fell to S_3 in year 3, then, to prevent the price rising above the ceiling level, ab would be released from the buffer stock.

Critique of buffer stock schemes

In practice, many problems are associated with these schemes:
- If the floor price is set too high, then there will be surpluses each year.
- Equally, if the ceiling price is set too low, then there may be insufficient stocks available in years of shortage.
- The schemes involve costs of storage.
- Success depends on ensuring that all the major producers agree to be part of the scheme and that none of them cheats, e.g. by selling to a major consumer at a reduced price.

Other strategies

Industrialisation: the Lewis model

It has traditionally been assumed that development is synonymous with industrialisation, i.e. that development requires an increasingly large manufacturing sector. The structural change/dual sector model (the Lewis model) is based on the view that development requires a move away from traditional agriculture (characterised by subsistence, low productivity and barter) to more productive manufacturing (characterised by high productivity and monetary exchange).

> **Buffer stock scheme**
> A way of reducing price fluctuations. It involves setting a ceiling and a floor price and the buying and selling of stocks to maintain price within these limits.

> **Exam tip**
> The analysis is more straightforward if the supply is assumed to be perfectly inelastic. This is a reasonable assumption because a set amount will be produced each year.

> **Knowledge check 19**
> Give two examples of market-orientated strategies and two examples of interventionist strategies to promote growth and development.

Emerging and developing economies

Key features of the Lewis model
- This model describes the transfer of surplus labour from a low productivity (subsistence) agricultural sector to a high productivity industrial sector.
- Lewis thought that, because of the excess supply of workers, the marginal productivity (MP) of agricultural workers might be zero or close to zero. This is based on the **law of diminishing returns** (see Theme 3).
- With MP at zero, then the opportunity cost of transferring workers from the agricultural sector to the industrial sector would be zero.
- Industrialisation will be associated with investment (possibly from transnational companies), which will increase productivity and profitability. If profits are reinvested, then further growth will occur.
- The share of profits as a percentage of GDP will increase, as will the savings ratio, providing more funds for investment and continued economic growth.

Law of diminishing returns This states that, when successive units in a variable factor of production are added to fixed factors, the marginal product will eventually decrease.

Criticisms of the Lewis model
- Profits made in the industrial sector might not be invested locally, especially if firms are owned by transnational companies.
- Reinvestment might be made in capital equipment, with the result that only a limited amount of extra labour is required.
- Empirical evidence suggests that the assumption of surplus labour in the agricultural sector and full employment in the industrial sector is invalid, e.g. favelas in South America.

Development of tourism

Tourism has played a significant part in the process of development of many countries including Tanzania, Vietnam and the Seychelles. There are advantages to this strategy over primary product dependency, not least that demand is likely to be *income elastic*. The expansion of tourism has strong attractions for developing countries.

Advantages associated with the development of tourism
- It is a valuable source of foreign currency as tourists spend money on goods and services provided within the local economy.
- Tourism is likely to attract investment by transnational hotel chains.
- In turn, this will increase GDP via the multiplier.
- Jobs will be created, both as a direct result of the investment in the tourist and leisure industries and also as a result of the multiplier effects within the economy.
- All of the above will help to increase tax revenues for the government, which may be used to improve public services.
- Tourism can help to preserve the national heritage of the country.
- Improvements in infrastructure may be made (e.g. a transnational company provides new roads as part of its contract to build hotels).

Disadvantages associated with tourism
- It may be associated with a significant increase in imports, not only for the capital equipment required to build hotels and facilities but also to meet the demands of tourists for specialist foods and goods. Further, the balance of payments on current account might be adversely affected by the repatriation of profits to shareholders of TNCs.

Content Guidance

- In times of recession, the fall in demand for tourism may be proportionately more than the fall in real income, assuming that demand is income elastic.
- Employment may only be seasonal in nature. Further, the jobs created may only be low skilled and low paid if the TNC supplies its own managers and professional staff.
- Tourism is subject to changes in fashion. In the developed world, Spain has suffered from a significant downturn in tourism in recent years, as Europeans now prefer more exotic destinations. Further, terrorist incidents in countries such as Turkey and Egypt led to a significant fall in the number of tourists.
- There may be significant *external costs* (e.g. increase in waste, pollution of beaches, water shortages for local people) as the needs of tourists are prioritised. The damage to the environment caused by tourists might result in restrictions (e.g. the restrictions on the number of tourists allowed each day on the Galápagos islands; visitors to Machu Picchu are limited by the requirement to have a guide).

> **Knowledge check 20**
> How might foreign currency earned from tourism stimulate economic development?

Development of primary industries

Some developing countries have achieved growth and development on the basis of investing in primary industries. The case for focusing on agriculture and hard commodities is that the country may have a comparative advantage in the production of these goods and so resources are more efficiently allocated to that use. Such a comparative advantage should be viewed in a dynamic context (i.e. as the country experiences growth, the government may use its tax revenues to spend on education). As a result of such a dynamic process, the country may gain a comparative advantage in other products.

Some countries have specialised in producing primary products with a high income elasticity of demand, e.g. Peru produces asparagus; Chile produces blueberries, wine and papaya; Bolivia produces tin. Consequently, during periods of world economic growth, they have benefited from significant increases in demand.

Fair trade schemes

The aim of fair trade schemes is 'to address the injustice of low prices' by guaranteeing that producers receive a fair price. It means paying producers an above-market price for their produce, provided they meet particular labour and production standards. This premium is passed back to the producers to spend on development programmes.

The market for fair trade products has been growing rapidly and there are now over 2,500 product lines, including chocolate, tea, coffee, bananas, wine and clothes.

Advantages of fair trade schemes
- Producers receive a higher price.
- Extra money is available to spend on education, health, infrastructure, clean water supplies, conversion to organic farming and other development programmes in the producers' countries.
- There are smaller price fluctuations, allowing producers to be shielded from market forces.
- The extra money can also be used to improve the quality of products.
- Producers are enabled to diversify into other products.

Criticisms of fair trade schemes

- Distortion of market forces. Low prices may have resulted from overproduction which, in a free market, would act as a signal to producers to grow other crops. In addition, the artificially high fair trade prices encourage more producers to enter the market, so reducing prices for those not covered by the scheme.
- Certification is based on normative views on the best way to organise labour, e.g. in the case of coffee, certification is only available to cooperatives of small producers.
- Guaranteeing a minimum price provides no incentive to improve quality.
- These schemes are an inefficient way to get money to poor producers: consumers pay a large premium for fair trade goods but much of this goes to supermarkets in profits. Only 10% of the premium paid for fair trade coffee trickles down to the producer.
- The schemes may create a dependency trap for producers.

Aid

The term 'aid' is used to describe the voluntary transfer of resources from one country to another or to loans given on concessionary terms (i.e. at less than the market rate of interest). Official development assistance relates specifically to aid provided by governments and it excludes aid given by voluntary agencies. Aid may also be given for emergency relief (e.g. in the case of natural disasters or for the support of refugees during a civil war). The UN goal for the amount of aid offered by developed countries (agreed in 1970) is 0.7% of GDP.

There are various types of aid:

- *Tied aid*. This is aid with conditions attached (e.g. there might be a requirement to buy goods from the donor country or the aid might be given on condition that there are some economic and political reforms).
- *Bilateral aid*. This is aid given directly by one country to another.
- *Multilateral aid*. This occurs when countries pay money to an international agency such as the World Bank which then distributes it to countries on the basis of certain criteria.

Knowledge check 21

What is the difference between aid and FDI?

The arguments in favour of aid include:

- A reduction in absolute poverty.
- Filling the savings gap experienced by many developing countries (this may be related to the Harrod–Domar model).
- To fill the foreign exchange gap so enabling countries to buy imports, e.g. capital equipment.
- Providing funds for infrastructure — essential if the country is to industrialise. Aid, therefore, will help to increase aggregate demand and investment will have a multiplier effect on GDP.
- Improving human capital through promotion of healthcare, education, training and expertise (e.g. the training of teachers and doctors).
- Possible contribution to increased globalisation and trade, both of which are frequently associated with growth and development.
- A reduction in inequality between countries.

Content Guidance

There are powerful arguments against the use of aid, except in the case of emergency aid, some of which are listed below:
- It results in a dependency culture (i.e. the recipients of aid become dependent on it and do not, therefore, pursue appropriate macroeconomic policies to achieve independent growth and development).
- Aid might not benefit those for whom it is intended (e.g. it could be diverted into military expenditure or it could be 'lost' as a result of corruption).
- There is no clear evidence that aid contributes to the reduction of absolute poverty or to growth and development.
- Right-wing economists argue that aid distorts market forces and results in an inefficient allocation of resources, while left-wing economists regard aid as a form of economic imperialism by which donor countries aim to secure political influence in the countries to which they give aid.
- Aid in the form of concessional loans involves the repayment of interest, in which case there will be an opportunity cost for the developing countries, e.g. improvements in the health and education services.

Debt relief

The burden of debt bears heavily on some countries, e.g. Gambia, Mali, Nicaragua, Bolivia and Malawi.

The debt is usually owed to all or some of the following: the IMF, the World Bank, governments and banks in the developed countries.

The problem is that servicing the debt (i.e. paying the interest on the debt) may account for a disproportionate amount of public expenditure, to the extent that resources available for expenditure on health and education are severely limited. As a result, pressure to cancel the debts of the poorest countries has increased. Under the Heavily Indebted Poor Countries (HIPC) initiative and the Multilateral Debt Relief Initiative (MDRI), the World Bank provides debt relief to the poorest countries of the world. The HIPC initiative was started in 1996 by the IMF and World Bank with the aim of reducing the external debts of the poorest and most heavily indebted countries of the world to sustainable levels. In 2005, the HIPC initiative was enhanced by the MDRI in order to speed up progress towards meeting the Millennium Development Goals (MDGs). Forty-one countries were identified as being eligible for HIPC initiative assistance and, of these, 36 countries had benefited from HIPC and MDRI debt relief by 2015.

Arguments for debt cancellation
- Developing countries would have more foreign currency with which to buy imported capital and consumer goods from the developed countries.
- To the extent that the money released from debt cancellation is used for the purchase of capital goods, then there is the prospect of higher economic growth in the future.
- In turn, this means that developing countries would be able to buy more goods from richer countries.
- It could help to reduce absolute poverty.
- It could help to reduce both the savings gap and the foreign exchange gap.
- It might help to conserve the environment, e.g. 'debt for nature swaps'.

Knowledge check 22
What is meant by debt servicing and why is it significant?

Emerging and developing economies

Arguments against the cancellation of debt
- In comparison with aid, it is likely to take much longer to agree a debt cancellation programme.
- Unless conditions are attached to debt cancellation, there is no guarantee that the governments of these countries will pursue sound macroeconomic policies (i.e. there a moral hazard problem).
- Corruption might mean that the benefits of debt cancellation are channelled to government officials rather than to the poor.
- Shareholders of banks in the developed world may bear some of the burden of debt cancellation.
- It may be much less effective than the introduction of policies to reduce protectionism in developed countries.

Knowledge check 23
Why might there be a moral hazard problem if debts of developing countries are cancelled?

Exam tip
The arguments for and against debt cancellation are very similar to those for aid.

Awareness of international institutions and non-governmental organisations (NGOs)

The World Bank

The original role of the World Bank was to provide long-term loans for reconstruction and development to member nations that had suffered in the Second World War. However, in the 1970s, its role changed to cover setting up agricultural reforms in developing countries, giving loans and providing expertise. It is now focused on providing loans for projects that are designed to encourage economic development. For example, finance is directed towards healthcare, broadening education and infrastructure. In addition, loans are given to local communities and households to help them to develop micro-businesses. Overall, the World Bank has funded over 12,000 development projects through traditional loans, interest-free credit and grants since 1947.

Exam tip
Use case study material in your examination answers. The World Bank website (www.worldbank.org) provides detailed information on countries.

International Monetary Fund (IMF)

Established after the Second World War, the original role of the International Monetary Fund (IMF) was to increase international liquidity and to provide stability in capital markets through a system of convertible currencies pegged to the dollar. It allowed countries with balance of payments deficits to borrow money temporarily and repay their debt to others. The hope was that this would create financial stability, foster global cooperation and facilitate trade and growth, as well as reducing poverty.

In the 1970s, there were significant oil price shocks and many countries — especially developing countries — suffered from rapid inflation, huge balance of payments deficits and debt crises. As a result, most currencies were allowed to float (i.e. the peg to the dollar was broken). The IMF extended its role to include involvement in economic development and poverty reduction. To ensure repayment of loans, the IMF imposed restrictions and conditions on the economic policies to be followed by developing countries — *stabilisation programmes* — to achieve internal and external balance. In practice, these programmes were based on free market reforms, e.g. trade liberalisation, removal of state subsidies, privatisation, floating exchange rates and measures to reduce budget deficits.

Theme 4 A global perspective

Content Guidance

In 2006, the IMF was given a new role: namely, to conduct multilateral surveillance of the global economy and to suggest steps that the leading nations should take to promote it. It was also required to ensure more balanced growth and to reduce global imbalances.

The IMF is funded by quotas from countries, based on their GDP. Up to a quarter of the quota is payable in dollars, euros, yen or sterling or *special drawing rights* (SDR) and the other three-quarters in the country's own currency. In 2010, it was agreed that the IMF's quota resources would be doubled in order to deal with new demands resulting from the global financial crisis. Countries that have borrowed from the IMF since the 2008 financial crisis include Greece, Iceland, Hungary and Ukraine. More recently Sri Lanka borrowed $1.5bn to avert a balance of payments crisis in 2016 while in 2018 Argentina was bailed out with the largest ever loan in IMF history ($50bn).

> **Knowledge check 24**
>
> Why did countries such as Greece, Ireland and Portugal need to borrow from the IMF after 2010?

The future of the World Bank and the IMF

The roles of the IMF and the World Bank are currently blurred: both have a role in the developing world and in poverty reduction and it is suggested that they should be reformed to reflect the changing needs of the global economy. Critics of the institutions as they currently operate suggest the following:

- The IMF should be slimmed down and should undertake short-term lending to crisis-hit countries.
- The World Bank should act as a development agency and undertake a detailed credit appraisal of the creditworthiness of recipient countries.

NGOs

The work of non-governmental organisations (NGOs) has brought *community-based development* to the forefront of strategies to promote growth and development (i.e. the focus has moved away from state-managed schemes). The key characteristics of these community-based schemes are:

- local control of small-scale projects
- self-reliance
- emphasis on using the skills available
- environmental sustainability

Examination skills and concepts

- Understanding the complex nature of economic development and its distinction from economic growth.
- Understanding of the different ways by which development might be measured.
- Assessment of the significance of factors influencing growth and development with particular reference to concepts such as the savings gap, the foreign exchange gap, capital flight and primary product dependency.
- Ability to evaluate a range of strategies to promote growth and development and to be able to differentiate between market-orientated strategies and interventionist strategies.
- Ability to give examples from specific countries to illustrate the points made. This skill may be gained by adopting a case-study approach.
- Evaluation of the roles of the IMF, the World Bank and NGOs

Emerging and developing economies

Common examination errors
- Confusion between growth and development.
- Not providing examples to illustrate the point being made.
- Confusion between aid and FDI.
- Assumption that measures to increase economic growth will automatically result in development.

Links and common themes
- Primary product dependency may be illustrated using supply and demand analysis covered in Theme 1. Further, analysis of this issue involves the application of price elasticities of demand and supply and also income elasticity of demand.
- Market-based and interventionist policies link with supply-side policies covered in Theme 2.
- In discussing the strategies, it is often appropriate to employ *AD/AS* analysis, e.g. in considering the impact of aid (see Theme 2).
- The market-orientated strategies link with the market economics covered in Theme 1.

Summary
- There are several ways of measuring development such as the human development index (HDI).
- There is a range of factors that might influence growth and development in developing countries, one of the most significant of which is primary product dependency. This may be analysed by reference to the Prebisch–Singer hypothesis.
- Other factors affecting growth and development include: insufficient saving and foreign currency, fluctuations in commodity prices, capital flight, population issues, debt, access to credit and banking, education and skills, and unallocated property rights.
- Non-economic factors influencing growth and development include corruption, wars and political instability.
- There are many ways in which developing countries could achieve growth and development, including: market-orientated strategies, e.g. trade liberalisation, floating exchange rates and privatisation; interventionist strategies, e.g. protectionism, managed exchange rates and buffer stock schemes; and other strategies, e.g. industrialisation, development of tourism, aid, debt relief and fair trade schemes.
- The IMF, World Bank and non-governmental organisations (NGOs) can play an important role in promoting growth and development.

Content Guidance

The financial sector

Role of financial markets

To facilitate saving
A traditional role of the banks and other financial institutions, e.g. insurance companies and pension funds, is to provide facilities for individuals and firms to save, so enabling them to purchase goods at a later date.

To lend to businesses and individuals
A function of banks and other financial institutions is to provide credit. Without this facility, individuals and businesses may have cash flow problems.

To facilitate exchange
Transfers of money can be arranged easily when there is a fully developed banking and financial system. With the growth of online banking and smart debit cards, most such transfers now occur electronically.

To provide forward markets in currencies and commodities
The foreign currency and commodity markets provide forward markets for currencies and commodities so that traders can buy in advance, so reducing risks associated with the price volatility that often characterises such markets.

To provide a market for equities
Stock exchanges enable stocks and shares to be traded. This enables companies to raise money and provides an opportunity for investors to purchase shares.

Market failure in the financial sector

Asymmetric information
Financial markets and the products they deal with have become increasingly complex over recent years.

Externalities
Failure of financial institutions may have undesirable spillover effects (external costs) on third parties who are not directly involved in the financial sector. For example, the failure of a bank might result in bankruptcies for other businesses if it means that bank customers lose their deposits and can no longer pay their bills to other businesses.

Externalities Costs or benefits to third parties not part of the transaction. If externalities exist, there would be a divergence between social costs/benefits and private costs/benefits.

Moral hazard
During the financial crisis of 2008 the UK government rescued several banks, including Northern Rock, RBS and Lloyds. They were regarded by many as 'too big to fail'. However, some argued that this created a moral hazard because other banks and financial institutions would know that, in times of difficulty, the government would step in to prevent them from going bankrupt. There is a danger, therefore, that they will continue to pursue risky lending and investments.

The financial sector

Speculation and market bubbles

Between 2000 and 2007, UK banks created £1 trillion, doubling the amount of money and debt in the economy, but only 8% of this went to business. Over half went to residential and commercial property and 32% to the financial sector. This extra money in the economy helped to fuel bubbles in the property markets and eventually debts related to these bubbles became unpayable.

Market rigging

Market rigging occurs when some of the companies in a market act together to stop a market working freely in order to gain an unfair advantage.

In 2015, several major banks around the world were fined for manipulation of Libor, the global benchmark interest rate. For example, Deutsche Bank, Germany's largest bank, was fined a record $2.5bn for rigging Libor and was ordered to sack seven employees.

Also, Barclays was fined £1.5bn after rogue traders were caught manipulating foreign currency rates.

Role of central banks

Implementation of monetary policy

Central banks are usually responsible for controlling the cost and supply of money. In this role they set interest rates, and are responsible for asset purchases (quantitative easing) and sales.

Many central banks are now independent of their governments but may be required to make such decisions in relation to an inflation target.

Banker to the government

Most governments keep their accounts with the central bank of the country.

Banker to the banks

Central banks also provide banking facilities to the high street banks. In the UK all banks must keep an account with the Bank of England.

Role of regulation in the banking industry

Following the financial crisis, many central banks are responsible for enforcing new regulations designed to prevent the risk of banks requiring a bailout from their government. These regulations are incredibly complex. For example, the Basel III regulations are over 200 pages long.

Some key regulations are:
- the requirement for banks to split their retail banking business from their investment banking activities
- an increase in the amount of capital held by banks

Knowledge check 25

Outline the external costs which could result from the failure of a bank.

Exam tip

Refer back to work covered in Theme 1 on market failure and use this analysis in answering questions on market failure in the financial sector.

Theme 4 A global perspective

Content Guidance

Examination skills and concepts
- Ability to understand the role of financial markets in the economy.
- Ability to assess market failure in the financial sector with particular reference to the banking sector.
- Ability to evaluate the functions of a central bank in a country.

Common examination errors
- Confusing the role of central banks and that of retail banks.
- Assumption that financial institutions are only concerning with lending.

Links and common themes
- The market failures identified are applications of the concepts introduced in Theme 1.
- Monetary policy was considered in some depth in Theme 2.
- Many central banks are required to meet an inflation target set by the government, also considered in Theme 2.

Summary
- The financial sector plays a crucial role in any economy, not least in facilitating savings and making credit available.
- The financial crisis illustrated that market failures may be associated with the financial sector.
- A central bank plays a pivotal role in implementing monetary policy and in overseeing the whole financial sector.

The role of the state in the macroeconomy

Public finance

Figure 14 shows the key elements of public finance.

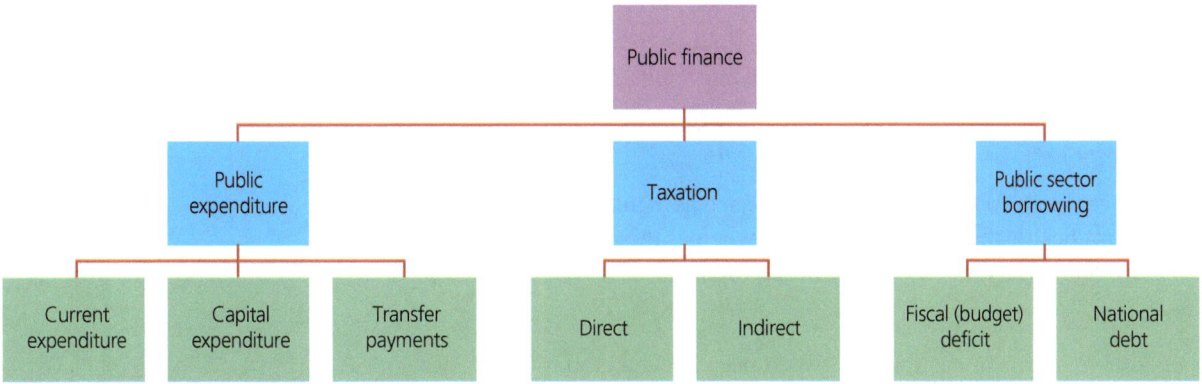

Figure 14 Key aspects of public finance

Public expenditure

Expenditure by central and local government can be categorised into three distinct types: capital expenditure, current expenditure and transfer payments.

Distinction between capital expenditure, current expenditure and transfer payments

Capital expenditure

This relates to expenditure on long-term investment projects such as new hospitals and roads. It is often referred to as *public sector investment*.

The objectives of public expenditure include the provision of public goods; defence and internal security; the provision of goods and services which yield external benefits and/or where there may be information gaps and asymmetric information, e.g. health and education; the redistribution of income; and expenditure to deal with external costs such as pollution and waste.

Current expenditure

This is day-to-day expenditure on goods and services, e.g. salaries of teachers and nurses, and drugs used by the NHS.

Transfer payments

These are payments made by the state (from tax revenues) to individuals in the form of benefits for which there is no production in return. Examples include child benefit, state pensions and the jobseeker's allowance. In the UK over a quarter of public expenditure is on transfer payments.

> **Exam tip**
>
> Transfer payments involve redistribution of income. Therefore they are not relevant to the calculation of a country's national income.

Content Guidance

Reasons for the changing size and composition of public expenditure

Factors influencing the size and pattern of public expenditure include the following.

The level of GDP

As incomes increase, so do expectations, and the demand for many government-provided services such as health and education rises more than proportionately because demand for them is *income elastic*.

The size and age distribution of the population

An increase in the size of the population (e.g. through immigration) is likely to place extra pressure on public services, while an ageing population will increase demand for medical services and social services for the elderly.

Political priorities

A government in a developed country might place particular emphasis on improving the quality of health and education services, whereas the priority of a government in a developing country may be to improve infrastructure.

Redistribution of income

Expenditure on those in *relative poverty* (see page 28) and on those with disabilities increased significantly in many countries before the 2008 financial crisis. However, subsequent austerity measures aimed at reducing fiscal deficits have led to cuts in *means-tested benefits* such as tax credits and housing benefits, resulting in an increase in relative poverty.

Discretionary fiscal policy

The 2008 financial crisis led to the resurrection of fiscal policy as a means of macroeconomic management in many countries, although often only temporarily.

Debt interest

The massive increase in fiscal deficits from 2008 led to sharp rises in national debts in many countries. For example, Greece's national debt as a proportion of GDP increased from over 125% in 2009 to 179% in 2018 while Italy's increased from 112.5% to 132% over the same period. In turn, this results in higher interest payments so that less money is available for public services.

The significance of differing levels of public expenditure as a proportion of GDP

Productivity and growth

Public expenditure on areas such as education, infrastructure and health might cause an increase in productivity and so result in a rightward shift in the long-run aggregate supply curve.

An increase in public expenditure will also cause an increase in aggregate demand because it represents an injection into the circular flow and so will have a *multiplier effect* on GDP. Therefore, higher public expenditure would cause an increase in economic growth.

> **Knowledge check 26**
> Approximately what proportion of UK public expenditure is spent on transfer payments?

> **Exam tip**
> When answering questions on this area it is useful to have current knowledge of the reasons for recent changes in the size and pattern of public expenditure.

The role of the state in the macroeconomy

Living standards
Higher public expenditure as a proportion of GDP could result in an increase in living standards if, for example, much of it went to the improvement of public services such as health and education, or to housing and infrastructure. However, this would not necessarily be the case if most went on defence or on interest payments on the national debt.

Crowding out
Increased public expenditure could cause crowding out. This might take two forms: resource and financial.
- *Resource crowding out* occurs when the economy is operating at full employment and an increase in public expenditure results in insufficient resources being available for the private sector.
- *Financial crowding out* occurs when increased public expenditure or tax cuts are financed by increased public sector borrowing, so increasing the demand for loanable funds and driving up interest rates.

Level of taxation
Countries that have relatively low public expenditure as a proportion of GDP may also have relatively low levels of taxation. Some economists consider that this is desirable on the basis that the state is less efficient at allocating resources than the free market; that it gives consumers more choice in spending decisions; and that growth tends to be higher in countries in which public expenditure does not rise above 35% of GDP. However, Scandinavian countries have high living standards despite public expenditure being a relatively high proportion of GDP, e.g. 48% in Sweden and 54% in Finland in 2017.

Equality
The impact of different levels of public expenditure on equality will also depend on the composition of that public expenditure. In countries in which public expenditure is weighted towards means-tested benefits, social housing, education, health and subsidies on basic food items, income distribution is likely to be more evenly distributed than in countries where public expenditure is weighted more to defence, universal benefits and prestigious investment projects.

Taxation
Distinction between progressive, proportional and regressive taxes
There are three broad categories of taxes: progressive, proportional and regressive.

Progressive tax
This is a tax in which the proportion of income paid in tax rises as income increases. Therefore, there are likely to be several tax bands, e.g. in the UK there were three bands in 2019, 20%, 40% and 45%' so that as income increases beyond a certain limit any further income is taxed at a higher tax rate.

Content Guidance

Proportional tax

This is a tax in which the proportion of income paid in tax remains constant as income increases. For example, some countries, e.g. Latvia, Estonia and Hong Kong, have a flat rate of income tax.

Regressive tax

This is a tax in which the proportion of income paid in tax falls as income increases. Although governments do not deliberately set regressive taxes, some taxes have a regressive effect, most typically those on expenditure.

> **Exam tip**
>
> Remember that the distinction between these categories of taxes depends on the relationship between the percentage of income paid in tax and taxable income.

The distinction between direct and indirect taxes

	Direct Taxes	Indirect taxes
What is being taxed?	Income and wealth	Expenditure
Where does the incidence of the tax fall, i.e. who bears the final burden of paying the tax?	A direct tax is paid by a person on whom it is legally imposed. Therefore, the burden of the tax cannot be shifted to any other person.	The burden of an indirect tax may be shifted in whole or in part from the person on whom it is imposed to a third party. For example, a business may be legally responsible for paying VAT but part or all of the burden may be passed on to consumers. Analysis of this was covered in Theme 1.
Examples?	Income tax, capital gains tax, corporation tax	Value added tax, excise duties, tariffs

The economic effects of changes in direct tax rates

Incentives to work

An increase in tax rates might have significant disincentive effects. For example, if the basic rate of income tax was raised, there would be less incentive for the unemployed or those not currently participating in the workforce to accept jobs. Similarly, if the higher rate of tax was increased, then people may be less willing to do overtime and more inclined to reduce their working hours, retire early or be less willing to seek promotion.

Tax revenues

Some economists consider that, if tax rates are increased too much, tax revenues may actually fall because the disincentives to work are so great. If the higher rate of income tax is increased, then there is likely to be an increase in tax avoidance (legal) and tax evasion (illegal) and a rise in the number of tax exiles. The Laffer curve illustrated in Figure 15 shows that, if the marginal tax rate is T then tax revenues will be maximised. However, an increase in the marginal tax rate to V will result in a reduction in tax revenues from R to S.

> **Knowledge check 27**
>
> How would an increase in income tax affect the opportunity cost of work?

The role of the state in the macroeconomy

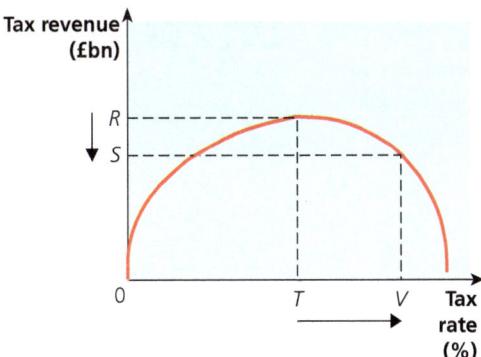

Figure 15 The Laffer curve

Income distribution

Most countries have a *progressive* income tax system so that the proportion of income paid in tax increases as income increases. Consequently, income tax makes income distribution more equitable.

Real output and employment

Figure 16 shows the effect of an increase in income tax. A rise in income tax would cause a fall in disposable incomes, which in turn would cause a decrease in consumption and, therefore, in aggregate demand. The disincentive effect of higher income tax rates could also cause the aggregate supply curve to shift to the left so real output would ultimately decrease from Y_1 to Y_2.

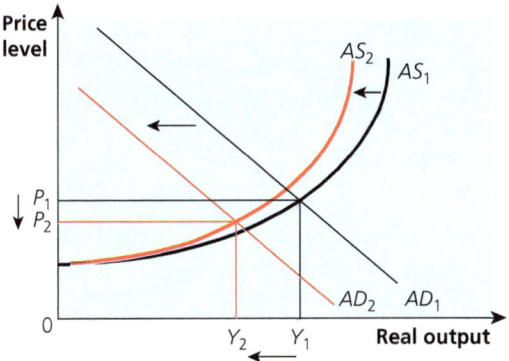

Figure 16 Effect of an increase in income tax rates

The price level

The fall in aggregate demand described above would tend to depress the price level, although this may be offset slightly by a leftward shift in the aggregate supply curve resulting from an increased disincentive to work.

The trade balance

An increase in income tax rates would cause a fall in disposable income. In turn, this would cause a reduction in consumption and, therefore, a fall in imports. This would result in an improvement in the trade balance.

FDI flows

Higher income tax rates might act as a deterrent to FDI because entrepreneurs and senior managers from the global company would face a decrease in their disposable incomes, assuming they would be based in the country for which the FDI was destined.

The economic effects of changes in indirect tax rates

Incentives to work

Indirect taxes have a less obvious impact on incentives to work than direct taxes. However, it is possible that an increase in indirect taxes would encourage people to work harder so that they can maintain their current standard of living.

Tax revenues

If VAT or other indirect taxes are increased then it is likely that tax revenues will increase. However, there is a danger that placing excessively high taxes on specific products might result in a fall in tax revenues. For example, high taxes on whisky resulted in less tax revenue, while high taxes on tobacco resulted in a considerable increase in smuggling.

Income distribution

Many indirect taxes have a *regressive effect*, i.e. people on low incomes pay a higher proportion of their incomes in indirect taxes than those on higher incomes. This is particularly true of specific taxes which are a set amount per unit. Consequently, indirect taxes usually make income distribution less equal.

Real output and employment

An increase in indirect tax rates would cause a fall in real income. In turn, this would cause a reduction in consumption. The *AS* curve would shift to the left because firms would supply less at any given price level. Consequently, real output and employment would fall.

The price level

An increase in indirect taxes will raise the price of most goods and services. If workers and trade unions respond by demanding wage increases to compensate for price rises, then an inflationary wage–price spiral could result.

The trade balance

An increase in VAT or excise duties would have no impact on the trade balance. However, an increase in tariffs would reduce imports and so result in an improvement in the trade balance.

FDI flows

Higher indirect tax rates might act as a deterrent to FDI because prices of finished products would be higher, so reducing the real income of consumers. However, if the product was primarily aimed at the export market, this may not be a significant consideration.

Exam tip

Include an aggregate demand/aggregate supply (*AD/AS*) diagram when considering the implications of changes in income tax.

Knowledge check 28

How is income distribution likely to be affected by an increase in income tax rates?

Other effects of an increase in indirect tax rates

- At a microeconomic level, an increase in indirect tax on a product would cause a leftward shift in the supply curve. The incidence of the tax on consumers and producers depends on the *price elasticity of demand* for the product (see Theme 1).
- The price of the product would increase above marginal cost, so resulting in allocative inefficiency, unless external costs are associated with the production of the product.

Public sector borrowing

Distinction between automatic stabilisers and discretionary fiscal policy

Fiscal policy refers to the use of government expenditure and taxation in order to influence the level of economic activity in a country. From the 1980s until 2008, its primary role was to ensure stable public finances. However, from 2008 it has once again assumed a role in macroeconomic management not only in the UK but also in China, the USA and a variety of other countries. Some key features of fiscal policy include the following.

- *Automatic stabilisers* relate to the fact that some forms of government expenditure and revenues from some taxes change automatically in line with changes in GDP and the state of the economy. These stabilisers help to reduce fluctuations caused by the trade/business cycle. Examples include progressive taxation and welfare payments such as unemployment pay and various means-tested benefits, e.g. pension credits for elderly people living on low incomes.
- *Discretionary fiscal policy* refers to deliberate changes in taxes and public expenditure designed to achieve the government's macroeconomic objectives. For example, the global economic crisis has led many countries to introduce a 'fiscal stimulus' to prevent severe recession. Typically, this has included: increases in public expenditure on infrastructure (roads and bridges in the USA), green technology and targeted subsidies to distressed industries (e.g. the car industry), and tax cuts.

> **Knowledge check 29**
> How would public finances be affected by a recession?

Distinction between a fiscal deficit and a national debt

A *fiscal (budget) deficit* occurs when public expenditure (both current and capital) is greater than tax revenues. Public sector net borrowing is the official term used to describe a fiscal deficit.

The *national debt* or public sector net debt is the cumulative total of past government borrowing.

Distinction between structural and cyclical deficits

The *'structural' fiscal deficit* is an estimate of how large the deficit would be if the economy was operating at a normal, sustainable level of employment and activity. However, it is difficult to estimate precisely what this 'normal' level would be.

The *'cyclical' fiscal deficit* is that part of the fiscal deficit associated with recession.

Content Guidance

Factors influencing the size of fiscal deficits

Factors influencing the size and pattern of public expenditure include the following:

- *GDP.* During a recession, real GDP will be falling. In turn, public expenditure on automatic stabilisers will be rising while tax revenues will be falling. Consequently, fiscal deficits will be increasing. In contrast, during a period of rising real GDP, public expenditure on automatic stabilisers will be falling while tax revenues will be rising and so fiscal deficits will be decreasing. However, the demand for many government-provided services such as health and education rises more than proportionately because demand for them is *income elastic*, putting upward pressure on public expenditure.
- *The size and age distribution of the population.* An increase in the size of the population is likely to mean an increase in public expenditure on health, education and infrastructure. An ageing population will lead to an increase in the dependency ratio, i.e. fewer workers per pensioner. This implies lower tax revenues from workers combined with higher expenditure on pensions to retired people, so causing an increase in fiscal deficits.
- *Discretionary fiscal policy.* The 2008 financial crisis led to the resurrection of fiscal policy as a means of managing the economy in several countries. (See page 61.)
- *Debt interest.* The massive increase in fiscal deficits from 2008 in the UK and many developed economies led to sharp rises in these countries' national debts (see below). In turn, this resulted in higher interest payments on the national debt.

> **Exam tip**
> When answering questions on this area it is useful to have current knowledge of the reasons for recent changes in the size and pattern of public expenditure.

Factors influencing the size of national debts

The national debt of a country would be affected by the factors listed above as well as the following:

- *Fiscal deficits or fiscal surpluses.* If a country had persistent fiscal deficits then the national debt would be increasing, whereas if there were persistent surpluses then the size of the national debt is likely to fall.
- *Unplanned events.* Wars and natural disasters might mean that the government is forced to increase its expenditure significantly. This would cause a deterioration in the public finances. For example, the UK's national debt was over 230% of GDP after the Second World War.

The significance of the size of fiscal deficits and national debts

Some argue that, if the money is being used to finance improvements in infrastructure and other capital projects, then a large national debt might be justified because it would be increasing a country's future productive potential, so making it easier to repay in the future. However, certain problems may arise:

- There is an *opportunity cost* for future generations. Interest payments on the national debt mean that less money will be available for public services.
- *Crowding out.* If the increasing size of the national debt is an indication of an increase in the size of the public sector, then resource or financial crowding out could occur (see page 57).
- *Danger of inflation.* If the rising national debt has been caused by successive fiscal deficits and/or financed by money borrowed directly from the central bank, then

there is a danger that inflationary pressures will develop, since injections will be rising relative to leakages.

In the long run, future governments might be forced to raise taxes and/or cut public expenditure so that the national debt can be reduced.

> **Exam tip**
>
> Be sure that you can assess the effects of an increase in the size of the national debt of a country.

Macroeconomic policies in a global context
Use of fiscal policy, monetary policy, exchange rate policy, supply-side policies and direct controls

Measures to reduce fiscal deficits and national debts

To reduce fiscal deficits and national debts a government might increase taxes and/or reduce public expenditure. However, there is a danger that such austerity measures might make the situation worse if the fall in aggregate demand caused by such measures causes a significant fall in real output. The higher unemployment associated with a fall in real output would cause tax revenues to fall, while public expenditure on means-tested benefits would increase.

Measures to reduce poverty and inequality

Governments could take a variety of measures to reduce poverty and inequality, including:
- increasing means-tested benefits
- increasing the progressiveness of the tax system, e.g. by increasing the rates of tax on higher incomes and/or by increasing the number of tax rates
- increases in the national minimum wage
- provision of subsidised housing for the very poor
- increased support for children from low-income families, e.g. free childcare for the under-5s; pupil premium (extra finance to schools based on the number of children from poor backgrounds)

Changes in interest rates and the supply of money

Changes in interest rates and the supply of money are part of *monetary policy*.
- *Interest rate changes.* These are used to influence the cost of money and, in many countries, to achieve the inflation target set by the government. For example, if the inflation rate is predicted to rise above its target, then the central bank would increase the base interest rate. However, the use of interest rates has various disadvantages, for example:
  - the full effect of an increase in the rate of interest takes between 18 and 24 months to work through the economy
  - business costs rise
  - the exchange rate of the currency may increase, making a country's goods less price competitive
  - if confidence is high, businesses and consumers may continue to borrow and spend
- *Changes in the money supply.* In recent years this has been achieved through *quantitative easing*. This relates to the action of the central bank in buying

government bonds and corporate bonds from the commercial banks and other financial institutions. This has the effect of increasing bank deposits, thereby allowing banks to lend more easily to private and business customers. However, some argue that this policy is unlikely to be effective if the banks are risk averse and remain unwilling to lend unless the loan is risk free. There is also the danger that the increased supply of money in the economy could unleash a serious bout of inflation (based on the monetarist belief in *the quantity theory of money*). An increase in the money supply could also cause a depreciation in the exchange rate which, in turn, would result in an increase in net exports and so increase aggregate demand.

- *Modern monetary theory (MMT)*. This theory suggests that a country with its own currency does not need to worry about accumulating too much debt because it can always print money to pay the interest on the debt. The only limit on government spending is the threat of inflation. However, this will not be a problem if there is enough spare capacity in the economy to meet growing demand.

> **Knowledge check 30**
>
> What factors might limit the effectiveness of expansionary monetary policy?

Measures to increase international competitiveness

Firms can improve the competitiveness of their products by investing in new capital equipment with the aim of raising productivity. They could improve the design and quality of their products through research and development.

Governments can try to improve international competitiveness through a variety of *supply-side policies*. Of particular relevance are the following:

- measures to increase occupational mobility, such as education and training schemes
- macroeconomic stability, e.g. a low and stable inflation rate; sound public finances; a relatively stable exchange rate; steady economic growth
- public sector reform aimed at reducing regulations
- improvements in infrastructure
- privatisation and deregulation
- incentives for investment, such as tax breaks if companies use profits for investment rather than for distribution to shareholders

It should be noted that international agreements are likely to prevent individual countries increasing their competitiveness by raising tariffs. For example, a member of a free trade area cannot simply introduce tariffs on goods from other member countries. Similarly, most countries are members of the World Trade Organization (WTO), whose rules prevent a country unilaterally imposing protectionist measures unless there is a justifiable case.

Further, it is not correct to suggest that 'the UK government could devalue its currency' because the pound is a floating currency. Also, since the Bank of England is independent, the government cannot directly engineer a depreciation in the exchange rate of the pound through a reduction in interest rates.

> **Exam tip**
>
> Refer back to what you learned in Theme 2 about supply-side policies and look out for new measures being introduced by governments.

Use and impact of macroeconomic policies to respond to external shocks to the global economy

Characteristics of external shocks

External shocks to the global economy may take a variety of forms. Examples include:
- a sudden increase in oil or other commodity prices

- a severe weather event such as a tsunami that has implications for the global economy or a long-lasting drought affecting crops across the world
- a major financial crisis that has repercussions for the global banking system
- wars and civil unrest that disrupt transport links
- cyber-attacks that have implications for global communications or energy supplies

Policy responses

The policy response will vary according to the situation and priorities of policymakers. It should be remembered from Theme 1 that economists are unable to conduct laboratory experiments so policies used at one time in one set of circumstances may have a different impact than exactly the same policy measures used at a different time.

In the 2008 financial crisis, there was a coordinated monetary policy response, which meant that many central banks slashed their base interest rates. In addition, many governments adopted a fiscal stimulus involving cuts in taxes and increases in public expenditure. These measures were designed to prevent a 1930s-style depression.

Measures to control the operations of global (transnational) companies

The regulation of transfer pricing

Global companies may own various subsidiary companies that adopt pricing policies for transactions between these subsidiaries that are aimed at minimising tax liability. They do this by ensuring that the most profit is made in countries where the corporation taxes are lowest.

Limits to government ability to control global companies

In practice, it is very difficult for an individual government to regulate transfer pricing without global agreements because many transnational (global) companies are 'footloose', i.e. they can move easily from one country to another to take advantage of lower operating costs, e.g. wages, corporation tax, labour and environmental regulations. Further, their investment decisions may have a significant impact on the economy of a country. Consequently, the fear of losing the investment of these companies may make an individual government unwilling to take unilateral measures to control them.

Problems facing policymakers when applying policies

Inaccurate information

Information regarding GDP, the balance of payments on current account and retail sales is notoriously inaccurate and subject to subsequent revisions. This may present problems for policymakers in devising appropriate policies, given that they may be working with data that do not accurately reflect the state of the economy.

Risks and uncertainties

Some commentators consider that the financial crisis has had long-term repercussions for savings and investment. Such uncertainties make the job of formulating economic policy more difficult for policymakers.

Similarly, there is considerable uncertainty about the possible long-run impact of quantitative easing in the eurozone. Some monetarist economists argue that it could risk unleashing a massive bout of inflation (because money supply is being increased), while others consider that previous experience in other countries suggests that it will have little effect on the economy.

Inability to control external shocks

Policymakers are usually unable to predict external shocks or their potential consequences. As a result, it may be difficult for them to formulate appropriate policy responses. Such external shocks could include a sudden and dramatic increase in oil and commodity prices, the exit of a country from the eurozone or from the European Union, or political conflict.

> **Exam tip**
> Supply-side policies may be particularly relevant when considering the topic of international competitiveness.

Examination skills and concepts
- Ability to apply synoptic concepts when considering the objectives of public expenditure and the use of taxes.
- Ability to distinguish between the different types of taxes and their effects.
- Ability to analyse the effects of a change in public expenditure or taxation.
- Ability to understand the difference between a fiscal deficit and a national debt.
- Ability to evaluate the causes and consequences of fiscal imbalances.
- Ability to evaluate the effectiveness of macroeconomic policy instruments (monetary, fiscal and supply-side policies) in the management of the economy.
- Understanding of the significance of macroeconomic policy in a global context, especially in the light of major global shocks, e.g. the credit crisis.

Common examination errors
- Weak definitions (e.g. stating that progressive taxes imply that the more you earn, the more you pay. This is imprecise, because it could be true of progressive, proportional and regressive taxes).
- Confusion over the meaning of public expenditure (it is expenditure by the government *not* expenditure by the public, i.e. consumers).
- Confusing a fiscal deficit with a balance of payments deficit on current account.
- Not addressing the question set (e.g. in questions demanding an analysis of an increase in public expenditure, it would be incorrect to focus the answer on the effects of tax increases to fund the extra public expenditure).
- Confusion between the different macroeconomic policy instruments, e.g. between fiscal and supply-side policies.
- Omission of *AD/AS* diagrams and analysis in discussing macroeconomic issues.
- Failure to consider the broader effects of the use of macroeconomic policies, e.g. the impact of interest rate changes on the exchange rates.
- Failure to explain the transmission mechanisms fully.

The role of the state in the macroeconomy

Links and common themes

There is plenty of opportunity to include concepts covered in previous themes in this section. In particular, Theme 4 builds on the material covered in Theme 2, so it is worth reviewing that carefully. The following are some examples:
- Link with demand-side and supply-side policies (Theme 2).
- Components of aggregate demand; economic growth.
- Discussion of *price elasticity of demand* (Theme 1) when considering the impact of an increase in indirect taxes or subsidies.
- Consideration of *opportunity cost* (Theme 1) when discussing public expenditure.

Summary

- The public sector plays a significant role in the macroeconomy in many developed economies. For example, in the UK, public expenditure was nearly 38.5% of GDP in 2018–19.
- There are three different forms of public expenditure: capital (on long-term projects such as roads), current (day-to-day expenditure) and transfer payments (expenditure for which there is no production in return).
- There are three different categories of taxes: progressive, proportional and regressive; and two distinct types: direct (on income and wealth) and indirect (on expenditure).
- The relationship between public expenditure and tax revenues is expressed in terms of a fiscal surplus or fiscal deficit.
- Fiscal policy involves the use of changes in public expenditure and taxation to influence the level of economic activity.
- Monetary policy involves the use of changes in interest rates and money supply to influence the level of economic activity.
- Supply-side policies are designed to influence the supply-side of the economy through increasing competition and incentives aimed at increasing productivity.

Questions & Answers

This section comprises two exemplar papers, one representing Paper 2 (Macroeconomics) and the other Paper 3 (Microeconomics and Macroeconomics).

■ Paper 2

Format for Paper 2

Themes 2 and 4 will be tested in Paper 2 of the examination. You will find that Theme 4 builds on Theme 2. It repeats ideas but goes more deeply into the detail and wider implications (global rather than just UK). You should therefore use your Theme 2 and Theme 4 books together in your preparation for Paper 2 to gain a firm understanding of macroeconomics.

Paper 2 of the A-level specification comprises 35% of the weighting for the A-level examination. The time allowed is 2 hours and the total mark for the paper is 100. There are three sections in the paper:

- **Section A (multiple-choice and short answers), worth 25 marks**: there are five questions divided into parts, one of which is a multiple-choice question. The other(s) require a calculation or explanation.
  - The command words used in this section are: **define, calculate, explain**.
- **Section B (data response) worth 50 marks**: there are five parts as detailed below. The command words used in this section are:
  - **Explain** (5 marks). This is assessed on a points basis, i.e. there are marks allocated for knowledge, application and analysis.
  - **Examine** (8 marks). This is also assessed on a points basis: there are 2 marks for knowledge, 2 marks for application, 2 marks for analysis, and 2 marks for evaluation.
  - **Assess** (10 marks). This is assessed on a levels-of-response basis. There are 6 marks for knowledge, application and analysis, and 4 marks for evaluation.
  - **Discuss** (12 or 15 marks). This is also assessed on a levels-of-response basis. In the 12-mark questions there are 8 marks for knowledge, application and analysis, and 4 marks for evaluation. In the 15-mark questions there are 9 marks for knowledge, application and analysis, and 6 marks for evaluation.
- **Section C (essay), worth 25 marks**. The command words used in this section are **evaluate** and **to what extent**. There will be a choice from two macroeconomic essays. The essay is assessed on a levels-of-response basis. There are 16 marks for knowledge, application and analysis, and 9 marks for evaluation.

In the exemplar paper that follows, the questions focus mainly on the content covered in Theme 4 but will be useful as a practice after studying the second year of the A-level course. Note that they have not been accredited for Edexcel but follow the format of those in the sample assessment materials (SAMs) and of those set from 2017.

Section A

Question 1 Economic development

The table shows selected economic data in 2017 for Guinea and Liberia.

	HDI value	Life expectancy at birth	Expected years of schooling
Guinea	0.46	60.6	9.1
Liberia	0.43	63.0	10.0

Source: United Nations Development Programme Human Development Reports

(a) Which one of the following may be deduced from this information? (1 mark)

    A GNI per capita (2011 PPP $) must be higher in Guinea than in Liberia
    B GNI per capita (2011 PPP $) must be lower in Guinea than in Liberia
    C The standard of healthcare and education must be better in Guinea than in Liberia
    D The Gini coefficient must be higher in Guinea than in Liberia

(b) Explain **two** reasons why the HDI might be a poor indicator of economic development. (4 marks)

Student answer

(a) A

(a) This is the correct answer because Guinea has lower life expectancy and expected years of schooling than Liberia but a higher HDI, so its GNI per capita must be higher than Liberia's.
1/1 mark awarded

(b) HDI takes no account of the distribution of income. If incomes are very unevenly distributed then there may be a high proportion of the population living in absolute poverty who cannot afford the basic necessities of life.

Secondly, the HDI takes no account of individual and political freedom which, according to Amartya Sen, is an essential aspect of economic development because freedom is important for improving the quality of life.

(b) The answer identifies two issues and provides a linked explanation of each.
4/4 marks awarded

Questions & Answers

Question 2 Exchange rates

The graph shows the value of the Argentine peso (ARS) against the US dollar.

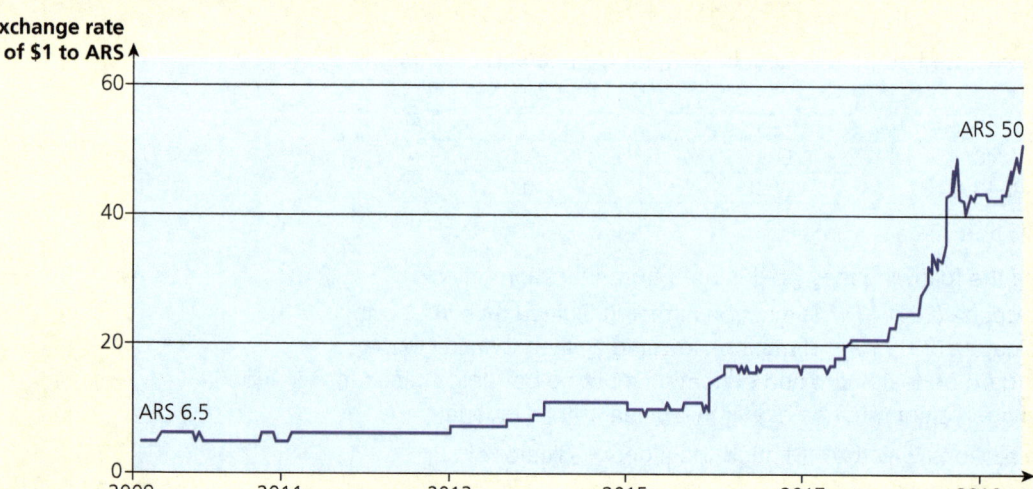

(a) Calculate the percentage change in the value of the Argentine peso against the US dollar over the period shown in the chart. (2 marks)

(b) Explain the effect of this change in the value of the peso on the international competitiveness of Argentinian goods. (2 marks)

(c) Which **one** of the following is likely to cause a depreciation in the exchange rate of a country's currency? (1 mark)
   - A There is an increase in the country's current account surplus
   - B There is an increase in foreign direct investment into the country
   - C The country's rate of economic growth is expected to increase
   - D The country's inflation rate increases significantly above that of its competitors

Student answer

(a) $\dfrac{43.5}{6.5} \times 100 = 669.23\%$

In other words, the value of the peso depreciated considerably against the dollar during this period.

(b) This will increase the competitiveness of Argentina's goods and services.

(c) D

(a) The answer shows the steps in the calculation, which is important because if a mistake is made in the calculation itself, marks may still be gained for the method. In this case the calculation is correct and is supported by a correct interpretation of the result. **2/2 marks awarded**

(b) The answer given is correct but it could be supported with a bit more reasoning. For example, it could be stated that the foreign currency price of exports would be lower while the domestic price of imported goods would be higher. **1/2 marks awarded**

(c) D is the correct answer because a higher rate of inflation would reduce the competitiveness of Argentina's goods and services so causing a fall in demand for Argentina's exports and, therefore, for pesos on the foreign exchange market. **1/1 mark awarded**

Paper 2, Section A

Question 3 Financial sector

(a) Which **one** of the following illustrates a market failure in the financial sector? (1 mark)
  A Provision of loans to businesses wishing to invest in new capital equipment
  B An increase in interest rates as a result of higher demand for loans
  C Excessive lending to individuals causing a rapid rise in asset prices
  D Banks accepting deposits by customers wanting a secure place for their savings

(b) Explain **two** methods by which a central bank might control the banking industry. (4 marks)

Student answer

(a) C

(a) Answer C is correct because this could cause a housing market bubble.
1/1 mark awarded

(b) A central bank could demand that retail banks could hold more liquid assets to ensure that they have sufficient funds in the event of a run on the banks.

Also commercial banks are required to keep a fixed proportion of deposits as reserves with the central bank. If the central bank increased this ratio, the power of the commercial banks to make loans would be reduced.

(b) Two methods are identified with some linked explanation of each. Remember that for 4 marks only brief explanations are required.
4/4 marks awarded

Question 4 Inequality

The following chart shows how the benefits of President Trump's tax cuts are distributed to American households in 2019.

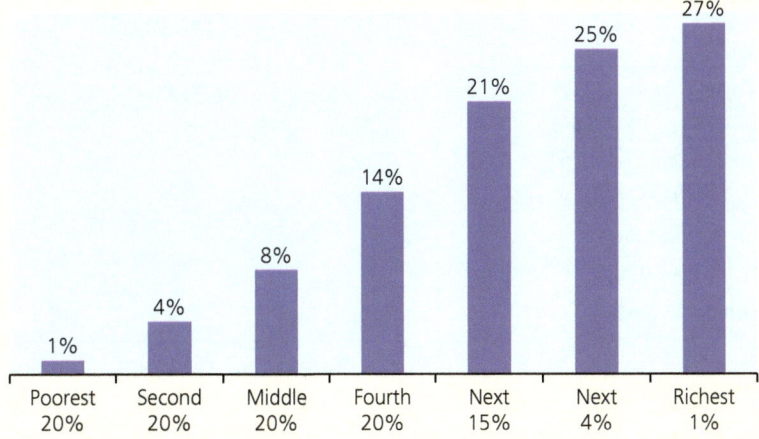

Source: Institute on Taxation and Economic Policy

(a) What might be inferred from the chart? (1 mark)
  A The USA's Gini coefficient would fall
  B The USA's Gini coefficient would increase
  C All households will suffer a fall in disposable income
  D Wealth in the USA will be more evenly distributed

Theme 4 A global perspective 71

Questions & Answers

(b) Explain what is meant by 'a progressive tax'. (2 marks)

(c) Explain the likely effect of a decrease in income tax rates on incentives to work. (2 marks)

> **Student answer**
>
> **(a)** B
>
> (a) The tax cuts have benefited those on higher incomes more than those on lower incomes. Ceteris paribus, income inequality would increase.
> **1/1 mark awarded**
>
> (b) A precise definition and an example from the UK tax system.
> **2/2 marks awarded**
>
> **(b)** A progressive tax is one in which the proportion of income paid in tax increases as income increases. For example, in the UK there are three rates of income tax: 20%, 40% and 45%.
>
> **(c)** A cut in income tax rates is likely to increase incentives to work.
>
> (c) The answer is correct but there is no linked explanation of why a decrease in income tax rates would increase incentives to work.
> **1/2 marks awarded**

Question 5 Terms of trade

Between January 2018 and January 2019, Singapore's import prices increased by 2.6% and its export prices rose by 0.3%.

(a) Given that January 2018 = 100, what was the value of Singapore's terms of trade in January 2019? (1 mark)

- A -2.3
- B 97.4
- C 97.76
- D 102.29

(b) Explain the likely effect of a decrease in Singapore's terms of trade on its trade balance. (4 marks)

> **Student answer**
>
> **(a)** C
>
> (a) C is the correct answer. To calculate the terms of trade the following formula must be applied:
>
> $$\frac{\text{index of export prices}}{\text{index of import prices}} \times 100$$
>
> **1/1 mark awarded**
>
> **(b)** If there is a decrease in Singapore's terms of trade it implies that import prices have risen relative to export prices. This would mean that Singapore's goods and services have become more competitive. In turn this should lead to an increase in Singapore's exports and a fall in imports.
>
> (b) This answer provides a clear chain of reasoning. However, the last link is missing, i.e. there should be a concluding sentence explaining that Singapore's balance of trade would improve.
> **3/4 marks awarded**

Section B

Question 6 The Gambian economy

Year	Gini coefficient
2000	47.3
2010	43.6
2015	35.9

Figure 1 Gini coefficients for The Gambia

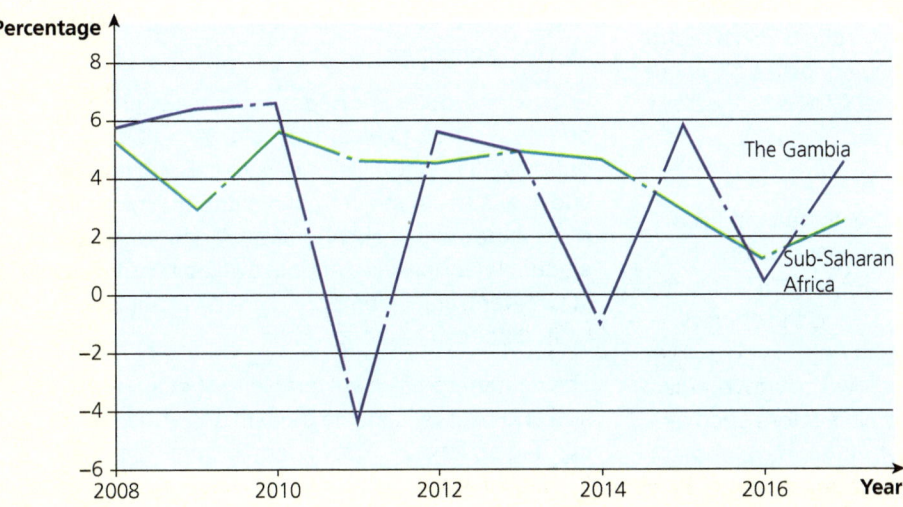

Figure 2 Annual real GDP growth rate (%) for the Gambia and sub-Saharan Africa

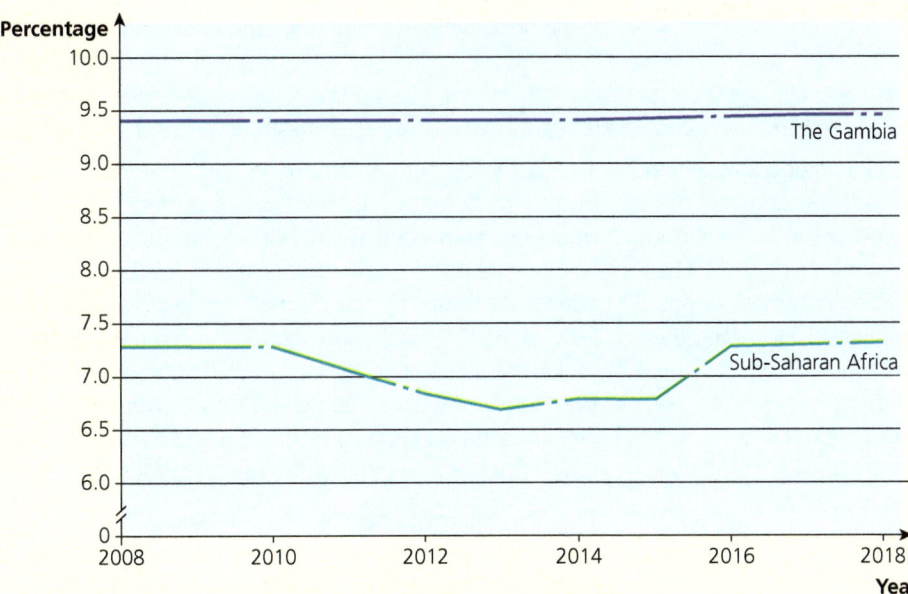

Figure 3 Unemployment rate for the Gambia and sub-Saharan Africa
Source, Figures 1–3: World Bank

Extract A Macroeconomic performance

After a sharp slowdown in 2016, real GDP growth was an estimated 5.4% in 2018, up from 4.6% in 2017, driven largely by services — tourism and trade, and financial services and insurance — which expanded by 10% in 2018. In tourism, the number of arrivals was expected to reach 225,000 in 2018 after surpassing its pre-Ebola peak of 171,000 in 2017. In addition there was strong growth in transport, construction and telecommunications. Short-term economic prospects are expected to steadily improve over the medium term with real GDP projected to grow by 5.4% in 2019 and by 5.2% in 2020.

The fiscal deficit fell to 3.9% of GDP in 2018 from 7.9% in 2017 as a result of increased fiscal discipline and foreign aid, and financial assistance from the IMF. However, the debt-to-GDP ratio stood at about 130% of GDP in 2017 and the country has been classified as being in debt distress. High public debt will continue to crowd out government spending in key socioeconomic sectors such as health, education and infrastructure development unless the government restructures its debt.

The current account deficit remained large — an estimated 19% of GDP in 2018, down slightly from 2017. The export basket contains mainly primary commodities, including groundnuts (55.6%), fish and fishery products (21.6%), and cashew nuts (10.6%).

Other challenges facing the country include a relatively high rate of inflation, a resurgence of political instability, the large increase in public spending, delays in implementing structural reforms, and adverse weather that could weaken rain-fed agriculture.

Energy and water shortages remain a vital policy priority. Access to electricity is 47% nationally but only 13% in outlying provinces. Such energy shortages make the cost of electricity among the most expensive in sub-Saharan Africa. Unreliable electricity supply also affects availability of water in Greater Banjul, compounding the problem of limited access to piped water.

The country remains vulnerable to shocks due to its size and over-reliance on tourism and subsistence rain-fed agriculture. Rapid demographic changes are fuelling intense urbanisation. The high share of youth unemployment in total unemployment, about 70%, is pushing young people to seek alternative means of livelihood, including migration and illicit activities.

Extract B Industry

The Gambian government has invested strongly in the agriculture sector because three-quarters of the population depends on the sector for its livelihood, and agriculture provides for one-fifth of GDP. The agricultural sector has untapped potential — less than half of arable land is cultivated. However, the sector faces several problems including:
- low and decreasing soil fertility
- low agricultural and labour productivity
- irregular rains that frequently cause crop losses
- a large proportion of unemployed or underemployed young people in rural areas
- high rates of emigration

Small-scale manufacturing activity features the processing of peanuts, fish and hides.

The Gambia's natural beauty and proximity to Europe have made it one of the larger tourist destinations in west Africa, boosted by government and private sector investments in eco-tourism. Tourism is booming and normally brings in about 20% of GDP, which is the second largest contributor to the national economy. However, it suffered in 2014 from tourists' fears of Ebola virus in neighbouring west African countries. Further, there is a need for new infrastructure to meet the needs of tourists.

The Gambia relies heavily on remittances from workers overseas and tourist receipts. Remittance inflows to The Gambia amount to about one-fifth of the country's GDP and remain the main source of foreign exchange earnings and are expected to increase by 5% a year.

Paper 2, Section B

(a) With reference to Figure 1, explain the effect of the change in the Gini coefficient in The Gambia between 2010 and 2015. Illustrate your answer with a Lorenz curve diagram. (5 marks)

> This question demands an understanding of Gini coefficients and the ability to use the data to draw a Lorenz curve that is labelled accurately.

(b) With reference to Extract A, examine two reasons why The Gambia's national debt may be a cause for concern. (8 marks)

> No more than two reasons should be identified with a fairly brief linked explanation of each. For application marks, reference should be made to the information provided. Since the command word is 'examine', some evaluation must be included.

(c) With reference to Figure 3, assess problems associated with The Gambia's rate of unemployment. (10 marks)

> Again, evaluation is required because the command word is 'assess'. Specific reference should be made to the data in Figure 3.

(d) With reference to the information provided, discuss constraints on economic growth in The Gambia. (12 marks)

> This question asks you to consider the constraints on economic growth. With a 12-mark question it is best to confine your answer to an examination of two or three issues so that there is time for sufficient analysis and evaluation.

(e) With reference to Extracts A and B and your own knowledge, discuss the case for the expansion of tourism as a means of promoting economic development in The Gambia. (15 marks)

> One way of approaching this question is to consider some benefits for The Gambia of expanding tourism and evaluate each one. It is important to relate these issues to economic development in The Gambia.

Questions & Answers

Student answer

(a) The fall in the Gini coefficient from 47.3 to 35.9 implies a decrease in income inequality. Consequently, the Lorenz curve will move closer to the line of equality (the 45 degree line). This is illustrated in the diagram below by movement of the Lorenz curve A to the Lorenz curve B, i.e. towards the line of equality.

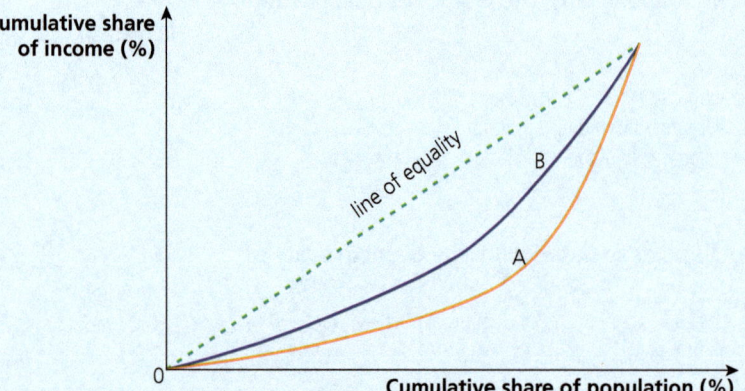

(a) This answer starts by making good use of the data and then analyses it with a clear explanation and an accurately labelled diagram.
5/5 marks awarded

(b) National debt is the cumulative total of past government borrowing. Large national debts occur when governments have persistent fiscal deficits. The government has to finance the national debt by issuing government bonds. ⓐ

In 2017 The Gambia's national debt was 130% of GDP. Such a ratio is usually considered to be unsustainable. A large and an increasing national debt would imply that more bonds must be issued which would drive down their price and increase their yield (interest rate). This increase in interest rates may lead to the crowding out of private sector investment because businesses would face an increase in the rate of interest on loans. It is argued that the private sector allocates resources more efficiently than the state due to the profit motive so there may be a welfare loss to society because the private sector firms are deterred from borrowing by the higher cost involved. However, some economists argue that the rising national debt might help to crowd-in private investment and provide jobs for the large numbers who are unemployed. ⓑ

A further reason that The Gambia's national debt may be a cause for concern is that debt interest payments will increase. This means there is an opportunity cost in terms of expenditure on, for example, health and education. Indeed, the country has been described as being in 'debt distress'. However, if the increase in the national debt is being caused by increased investment by the Gambian government on, for example, infrastructure then this may bring benefits to the Gambian economy in the longer term. ⓒ

(b) ⓐ The answer begins with an accurate definition of national debt, making it clear to the examiner that this key concept is understood. ⓑ The second paragraph considers one reason why The Gambia's national debt is a cause for concern with appropriate reference to the data and some evaluation in the last sentence. ⓒ The last paragraph offers a second relevant reason with reference to the extract and evaluation.
8/8 marks awarded

(c) The Gambia's unemployment rate is at least 2 percentage points higher than the average of countries in sub-Saharan Africa for the period 2008 to 2018. At just below 9.5% this implies that there is a large pool of labour not in gainful employment. a

One cost of such a high unemployment rate is that there might be an increase in emigration since about 70% of total unemployment comprises youth unemployment. This would reduce the productive capacity of the country and, therefore, could hinder economic growth in the long run. b

A further cost of unemployment is a loss of tax revenue for the government. Given that The Gambia has a fiscal deficit of 7.9% in 2017 and 3.9% in 2018 combined with a high national debt, such a loss of tax revenue is a serious issue for the government and would limit its ability to improve infrastructure, education and healthcare. c

(d) A distinction may be made between actual growth (which is usually defined as the increase in real GDP per year) and potential growth (an increase in the productive capacity of the country). a

One constraint on economic growth is over-dependence on agriculture. Extract 1 identifies several issues that might limit economic growth including 'low and decreasing soil fertility', low agricultural productivity and 'irregular rains that frequently cause crop losses'. Given that agriculture contributes 20% of GDP this is a significant factor that may constrain economic growth. According to the Lewis model it would be advantageous for a country to ensure labour is transferred from low agriculture (where productivity is low) to the more productive manufacturing sector. However, less than half of arable land is cultivated so there is the potential to expand this industry considerably and for it to contribute to economic growth. b

Another important constraint on economic growth in The Gambia is the lack of access to electricity which is just '47% nationally but only 13% in outlying provinces'. It has an adverse impact on agriculture because it 'affects availability of water in Greater Banjul'. Consequently irrigation may be impossible which would lead to crop failures. This could limit diversification from agriculture to manufacturing. c

Political instability is identified as another problem facing The Gambia. This is likely to deter investment both by domestic businesses and from transnational companies. d

(c) a Making reference to the data provides a good start to the answer. b This paragraph provides relevant consideration of the impact of high unemployment on emigration. It could have been enhanced by an *AD/AS* diagram to show the impact on productive capacity. c This paragraph contains a relevant explanation the tax revenue lost from high unemployment.

The main deficiency in this answer is that there is no evaluation. Given that there are 4 marks for evaluation, the maximum mark that this answer could achieve is 6/10. For evaluation it could be argued that the emigrants might return to The Gambia if economic prospects improve — economic growth is expected to be over 5% in 2019 and 2020. Further, those emigrating provide an important source of foreign currency in remittances, Indeed, remittances 'remain the main source of foreign exchange earnings and are expected to increase by 5% a year'.
6/10 marks awarded

(d) a It is useful to begin with a definition of economic growth. b This paragraph contains a relevant discussion of the country's dependence on agriculture as a constraint on growth with good application to the context provided. There is also some evaluation at the end. To improve further, the analysis could have been developed by considering issues such as price volatility and the income inelasticity of demand for many agricultural products. c There is a brief consideration of the problems of an irregular supply of electricity. However, there needs to be more detailed chains of reasoning and a more direct link to economic growth as well as some evaluation. d A brief point on political instability as a constraint on growth.

Overall, this answer would achieve only a Level 2 for knowledge, application and analysis and a Level 1 for evaluation.
6/12 marks awarded

Questions & Answers

(e) Economic development is a subjective concept referring to social and economic progress. One measure of economic development is the Human Development Index (HDI). It refers not only to GNI per capita but also to measures of health and education. **a**

Tourism may be a means to achieving economic development because 'The Gambia's natural beauty and proximity to Europe have made it one of the larger tourist destinations in west Africa.' The extract says that tourism accounts for about 20% of GDP. Tourism is an invisible export so an increase in tourism would act as an injection into the circular flow so resulting in a multiplier effect on GDP. However, the growth of tourism may create an increased demand for imports, for example, for capital goods to construct hotels and to meet the food needs of tourists. Further, it is stated that there is a need for new infrastructure to meet the needs of tourists which may involve extra public expenditure and the import of the necessary materials. **b**

Another argument for developing the tourist industry is that it creates employment for the population, especially important for The Gambia which has an unemployment rate of around 9.5%. The extra employment would also help to increase tax revenues for the government which would help to reduce the budget deficit of 3.9% of GDP in 2018. Further, the increased tax revenues could be used by the government to improve healthcare and education so contributing to economic development. However, much of the employment may be seasonal and in low-paid cleaning or waitressing jobs. Consequently, the living standards of the Gambian citizens may not increase very much. **c**

Tourism may suffer from unexpected events. For example, in 2014 it suffered from tourists' fears of Ebola virus in neighbouring west African countries. However, the number of arrivals was expected to reach 225,000 in 2018 after surpassing its pre-Ebola peak of 171,000 in 2017. Further, demand for tourism is income elastic: while the number of tourists might increase significantly during periods of strong global economic growth, there is likely to be a significant fall in the number of tourists during a global recession. **d**

(e) **a** The opening paragraph considers the meaning of economic development. **b** This paragraph makes an argument for the expansion of tourism making effective use of the information provided. There is some relevant evaluation at the end of the paragraph. However, the link to economic development is not made clear. **c** This paragraph considers the possible impact of tourism on employment. Again, there is appropriate reference to the information provided and a link to economic development. Some evaluation is also included at the end of the paragraph. **d** This paragraph explores some further dangers of a reliance on tourism as a means of promoting economic development.

Overall, the answer would score a low level 3 for knowledge, application and analysis, and level 3 for evaluation.

13/15 marks awarded

Section C

Question 7 Oil price increase

In the first 4 months of 2019 the world price of oil increased from $52 a barrel to over $70 a barrel.

Evaluate the likely economic effects of this increase in oil prices on the global economy. (25 marks)

> The command word indicates that evaluation is essential in answering this question. Its significance is illustrated by the mark allocation for this skill: 9 marks. There are 16 marks for knowledge, application and analysis.

Student answer

An increase in oil prices would affect the global economy because oil is essential in many parts of the production process for many goods. First, this would lead to a deterioration in the trade balances of oil-importing countries because demand for oil is price inelastic. This, however, would not be a problem for those countries that have large balance of trade surpluses or those who can finance trade deficits through surpluses in their capital and financial accounts. [a]

> [a] The answer begins by considering one impact of higher oil prices. This is a good strategy for a question of this nature where an introduction would be unnecessary. However, the explanation could have been developed more fully.

Higher oil prices are likely to lead to cost-push inflation as a result of a leftward shift in the short-run aggregate supply curve. This would cause a rise in the price level from PL_1 to PL_2 and a fall in real output from Y_1 to Y_2 as illustrated in the graph below:

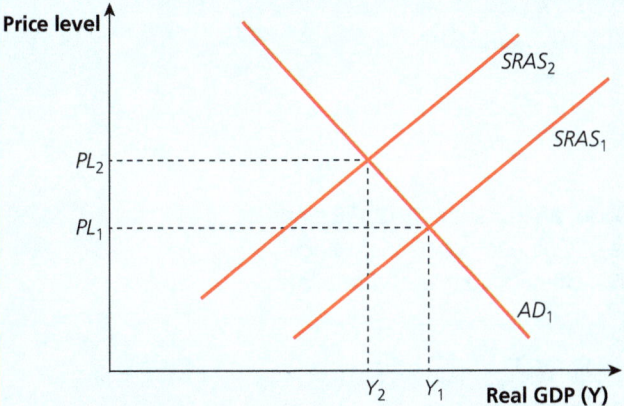

The increase in the price level would cause a decrease in real income so resulting in a fall in consumer expenditure. In turn, this could lead to firms' cutting investment causing a downward multiplier effect on GDP. [b]

The fall in consumption, investment and in real output would lead to an increase in unemployment. In turn, this would cause a fall in tax revenues and lead to higher welfare payments so causing a deterioration in the public finances. However, these effects might be less significant than in the past because many countries have been

> [b] There is good analysis of the possibility of cost-push inflation supported by an accurate AD/AS diagram.

reducing their reliance on oil as a means of energy production, for transportation and for manufacturing. c

In contrast to the impact on oil-importing countries, oil-exporting countries would benefit from the rise in oil prices since their export revenues are likely to increase so resulting in an improvement in their trade balances. Tax revenues in these countries are also likely to increase because the profits of the oil companies would be rising. Governments in oil-exporting countries might use these revenues to spend on public services. These injections from higher exports and increased government spending would have a multiplier effect on GDP so helping to increase the rate of economic growth. d

Developing countries dependent on oil imports might experience significant problems especially if they are dependent on agricultural exports. Indeed, oil imports of African countries make up around 10% of GDP, a much higher proportion than in developed economies. The larger import bill for oil might mean that some developing countries will have insufficient foreign currency for the purchase of other commodities or capital goods. This might reduce their economic growth rates and stifle development. Further, the higher oil prices will have a significant impact on the poor. Consequently, higher oil prices could increase inequality both between developed and developing countries and within countries. However, oil prices are often quite volatile. Therefore, the relatively high oil prices in the first few months of 2019 might only be temporary and so the above effects might apply in the short run only. e

c This paragraph develops the analysis from the previous point and includes some relevant evaluation which demonstrates a knowledge of changes in the global economy. d This paragraph provides a contrast with the previous discussion by considering the impact on oil exporting countries. This is sound but there is no evaluation of the points made. e There is sound analysis of the impact of higher oil prices on developing countries and some evaluation.

Although there is some evaluation, this answer lacks a concluding paragraph containing an informed judgement and so could only score a Level 2 for evaluation. Such a final paragraph might be on the following lines: 'Previous experience of oil price increases suggests that they have both an inflationary and deflationary impact on the global economy. In other words, there could be a period of 'stagflation' — in which there is both a high rate of inflation and a fall in economic growth and possibly a global recession.' The knowledge, application and analysis is just worthy of a Level 4.

19/25 marks awarded

Question 8 Trade war

In 2018 the USA's trade deficit with China was $419 billion, an increase of 12.1% since 2017. In May 2019 the USA increased tariffs on a range of Chinese goods including fish, handbags, clothing and footwear from 10% to 25%. China said it would retaliate by imposing tariffs on goods from the USA.

Evaluate the likely economic effects of such an increase in tariffs. (25 marks)

In these 25-mark essays evaluation is worth 9 marks and should include an 'informed judgement'. There are 16 marks for the other assessment objectives — knowledge, application and analysis. The focus of the answer may not just be on China and the USA but also on the global economy.

Paper 2, Section C

Student answer

Tariffs are a form of protectionism and are a tax on imported goods. In this case it is an ad valorem tax because it is levied as a percentage of the price of the product. **a**

Since China intends to retaliate with tariffs on US goods, one effect will be to reduce specialisation and trade. According to the law of comparative advantage, a decrease in specialisation and trade will lead to a fall in world output and, therefore, to a fall in living standards. However, the USA has argued that the tariffs are necessary because the Chinese government unfairly provides subsidies to its state-owned enterprises. **b**

The impact of an increase in tariffs on Chinese goods is illustrated in the graph below:

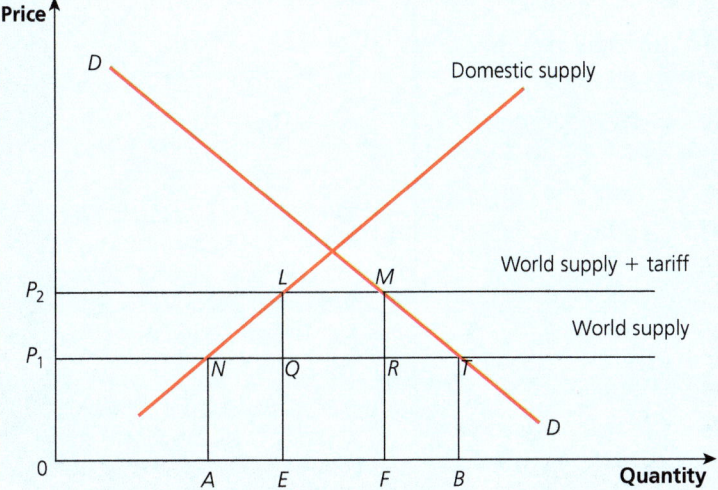

The price of Chinese imports would increase, so decreasing consumer surplus and increasing the producer surplus of US businesses. The higher prices of imports would lead to an increase in demand for domestically produced goods. The US government would gain revenue from the tariffs that could be used to improve public services such as education and healthcare. In contrast, Chinese manufacturers are likely to face a fall in demand for their goods with a consequent fall in revenues and profits. Further, some firms based in China might relocate to other countries to avoid the tariffs on Chinese goods. Both of these factors could lead to an increase in unemployment in China. **c**

a The student begins with a brief explanation of the meaning of tariffs.
b There is a relevant application of an important economic concept (comparative advantage) in this paragraph although its significance could have been explained more fully, perhaps with a numerical example.

c This paragraph includes a relevant diagram that is integrated well into the written analysis. To improve, there could have been some evaluation of the points made.

Questions & Answers

A major reason why the USA has increased tariffs on Chinese goods is because of its very large trade deficit with China. The higher tariffs were designed to reduce this trade deficit by making Chinese goods more expensive in the USA and so reducing demand for them. However, the impact of these tariffs will depend on the price elasticity of demand for Chinese imports. If demand is very price inelastic then the impact of the higher tariffs will be minimal. d

The US government may be hoping that the increase in tariffs would lead to 're-shoring', i.e. that American manufacturers might return to the USA to produce goods. However, it is more likely that they would relocate to other Asian countries that are not subject to tariffs such as South Korea, Taiwan and Thailand. Indeed, many Asian companies could transfer production out of China relatively easily. This factor, along with the overall impact of higher tariffs described above, is likely to lead to a higher rate of unemployment in China. However, China might be able to find new markets for its products in other countries so limiting the impact on unemployment. e

In the long run, most economists believe that the distortion of comparative advantage resulting from higher tariffs is likely to cause an overall fall in global economic growth, an increase in the rate of inflation and a higher rate of unemployment. However, there may be short/medium-term benefits for the USA in terms of an increase in economic growth and lower unemployment. This is because the tariffs should reduce the USA's trade deficit with China and lead to a stimulation of demand for goods produced in the USA. However, if China retaliates, then American citizens will face higher prices for imported goods with a consequent fall in real incomes and a slower rate of economic growth since demand for exports from the USA would fall. f

---

d A brief consideration of the likely impact on the USA's trade balance with China and some evaluation.

e A further valid point that has been supplemented well with the student's own knowledge. f The final paragraph brings together some of the arguments discussed and contains some 'informed judgements'.

Overall, this is a sound answer which includes relevant analysis and some good evaluation of a variety of issues.
22/25 marks awarded

Paper 3

Format for Paper 3

Paper 3 of the A-level is synoptic and covers content from all four themes. The paper consists of two sections, with each section containing one data-response question broken down into four parts. The last part of each of these data-response questions provides a choice of extended open-response essay questions and you will have to select one question from a choice of two. The total mark for the paper is 100, with each section worth 50 marks. Questions in both sections will require understanding of both microeconomics and macroeconomics. You will need to make connections between the content of this guide and that of the other themes. Therefore, you should use all four Student Guides to prepare for this paper.

In the exemplar paper that follows the questions focus on some of the content covered in Theme 4 but since this paper is synoptic it covers material from the whole specification. It will be useful for practice after studying the whole of the A-level course. Note it has not been accredited for Edexcel but follows the format of those in the sample assessment materials (SAMs) and of those set from 2017.

Paper 3 of the A-level specification comprises 30% of the weighting for the A-level examination. The time allowed is 2 hours and the total mark for the paper is 100. There are two sections (A and B) each with an identical format.

- Both sections A and B are worth 50 marks. The question in each of these sections has four parts with the following command words and mark allocations as follows:
  - **Explain** (5 marks: 2 for knowledge, 2 for application, 1 for analysis)
  - **Examine** (8 marks: 2 for knowledge, 2 for application, 2 for analysis, 2 for evaluation)
  - **Discuss** (12 marks: 8 for knowledge, application and analysis, 4 for evaluation)
  - **Evaluate** (25 marks from a choice of two: 16 for knowledge, application and analysis, 9 for evaluation)

Questions & Answers

Question 1 Italy's economy

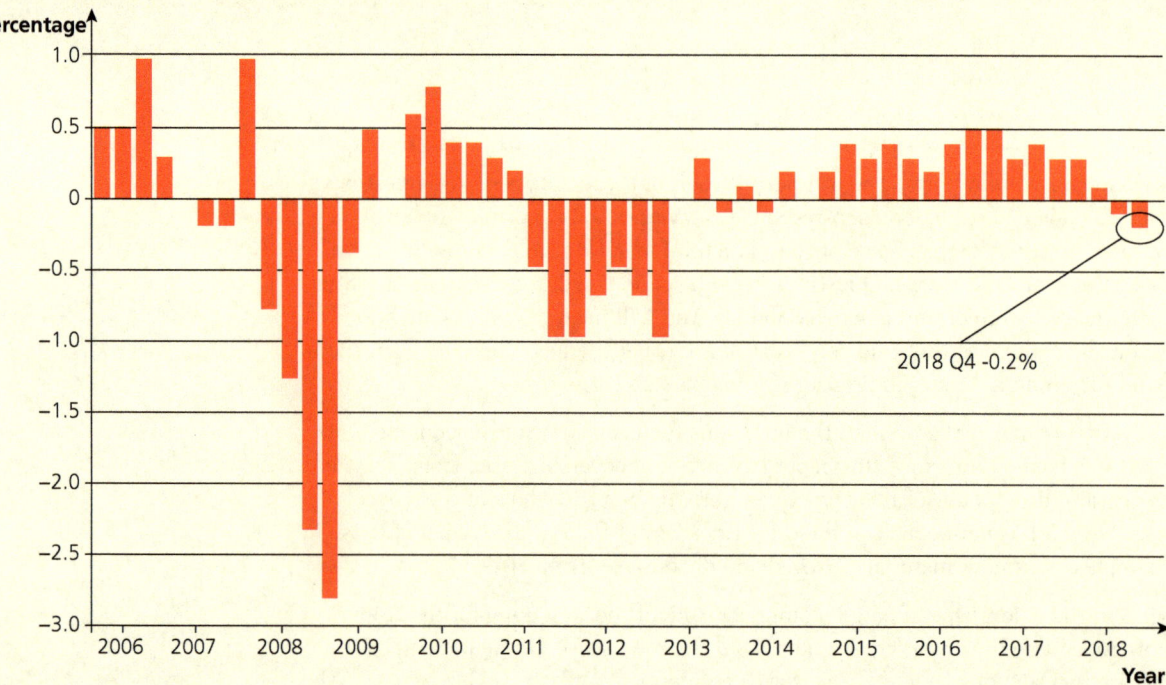

Figure 1 Real GDP quarterly growth, 2006–2018
Source: Macrobond, *The Independent*

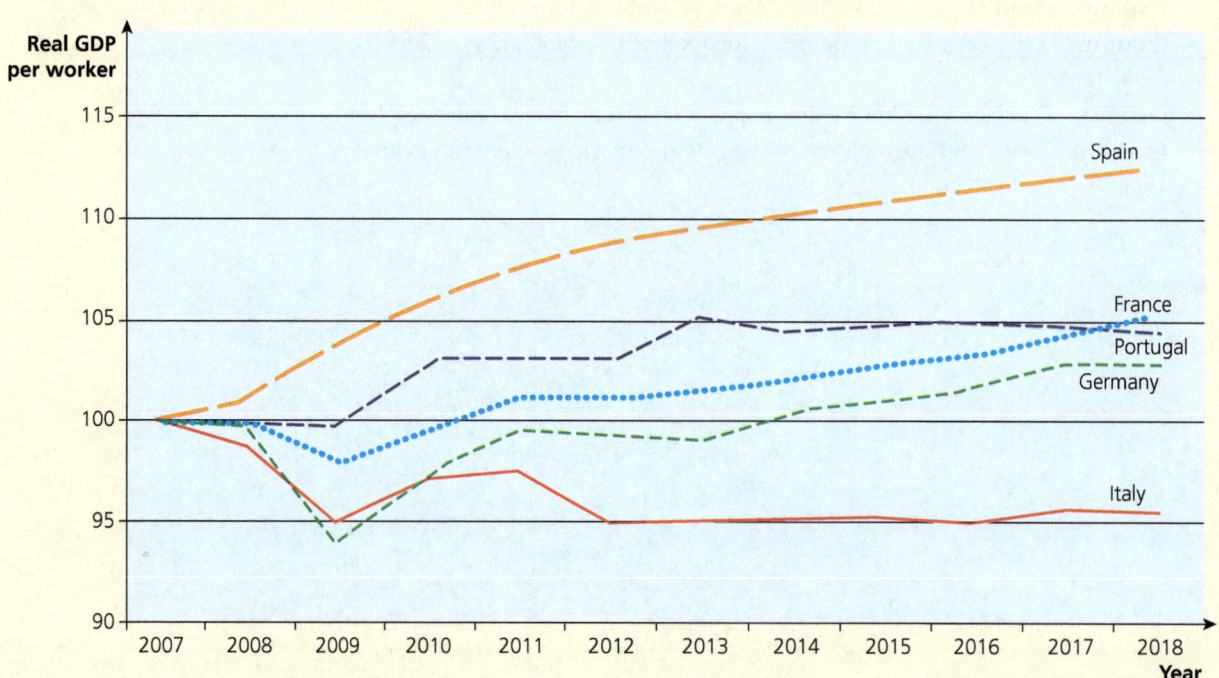

Figure 2 Real GDP per worker, 2007 = 100
Source: OECD

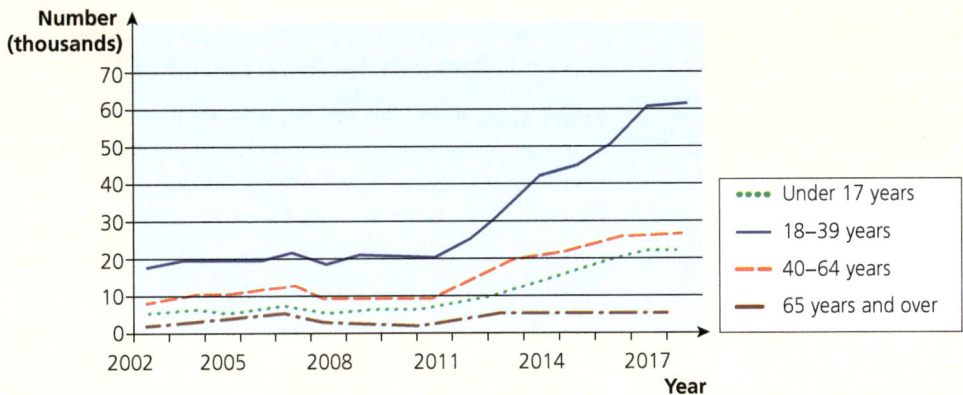

Figure 3 Emigration by age group, thousands
Source: OECD

Extract A Problems facing the Italian economy

Despite its size, Italy's economy is fundamentally very weak. In 2018, Italy went into a recession for the third time since 2008. Over the past 30 years its GDP has grown by an average of just 0.2% per quarter.

In 2019 Italy's economic output was still 5% below its pre-crisis peak of 2008. This resulted from very slow rates of economic growth (or negative growth) throughout this century. Consequently, real GDP per capita is less than in 2000. The data highlight the country's mediocre economic performance since the introduction of the euro in 1999–2002. Eurosceptics argue that the single currency is the primary cause of the economy's weak performance. They consider that devaluation could help to increase exports. However, other economists think that the country's problems are due to structural weaknesses, rather than the euro.

One problem is Germany's car industry. New regulations in 2018 forced a slump in production, and the sector has recovered only weakly. These German plants are important customers for the Italian factories that supply them with components.

Another concern is that Italy's national debt is more than 130% of GDP. High national debt is crowding out economic growth by attracting funds for government bonds that might otherwise have gone to more productive investment in the private sector. Interest on this debt was 3.7% of GDP in 2018 and this limited funds available for spending on infrastructure, healthcare and education. In the future it also could result in higher taxes on workers and businesses, and could destabilise financial markets.

Other problems included a combination of political turmoil, weak international growth and the long-term problems of Italy's banks that have restricted their ability to lend to businesses.

Investment was low as companies held off committing to any big financial decisions. This limited economic activity in the longer-term by reducing the amount of capital equipment available for production. In 2017 Italy was nineteenth of countries receiving foreign direct investment (FDI) even though it is the world's tenth largest economy in terms of GDP. Reasons why it was relatively unattractive for FDI include its very high national debt, increasing levels of corruption and restrictive employment legislation. Further, the Italian economy is heavily regulated, with access to many professions tightly limited. Many of the solutions (supply-side policies) are unacceptable to the population because they involve making employment less secure.

Questions & Answers

According to the European Commission 95% of Italy's businesses have fewer than 10 employees. OECD data show Italian companies of that size have lower levels of labour productivity than their peers. Larger companies also fail to innovate because of traditional family ownership which is unwilling to change, or because of the difficulty in obtaining credit. Another issue was that, in 2017, employer social security contributions were 24% of labour costs compared with the OECD average of 13%.

With regard to the labour force, fewer than one in three 25–34-year-old Italians has a university degree, well below the 44% OECD average. Italian 15-year-olds have lower maths, science and reading performances than most of their peers, according to the OECD PISA report.

(a) With reference to Figure 1 and to Extract A, explain the meaning of the term 'recession'. Use an *AD/AS* diagram to illustrate the movement of the economy into recession. (5 marks)

> This question demands clear reference to Figure 1 (examples of when Italy experienced a recession), followed by a written explanation and a diagram.

(b) With reference to Figure 2 and Extract A, examine two likely reasons for Italy's low productivity. (8 marks)

> It is a good idea to define productivity. Two reasons should be identified with linked explanations and appropriate use of the information provided. Finally, evaluation is required because the command word is 'examine'.

(c) With reference to Extract A, discuss the impact of differences in employer social security contributions in Italy compared with the average of OECD countries. Use a cost and revenue diagram in your answer. (12 marks)

> Again, evaluation is required because the command word is 'discuss'. It is also important to include a relevant diagram in the answer.

EITHER

(d) With reference to the information provided and your own knowledge, evaluate the likely microeconomic and macroeconomic impact on Italy's economy of changes in emigration. (25 marks)

> It is important to ensure there is both depth of analysis and breadth in the answer. In particular, both microeconomic and macroeconomic effects must be considered. It is also necessary to relate the analysis to the context of the question, i.e. the impact of emigration on the Italian economy. Given that 'evaluate' is the command word, the points considered should be evaluated and there should be a concluding paragraph containing an 'informed judgement'.

Paper 3, Section C

OR

(e) With reference to the information provided and your own knowledge, evaluate the microeconomic and macroeconomic impact of policies that could be used by Italy's government to reduce its national debt as a proportion of GDP. (25 marks)

> As with (d), it is important to ensure there is both depth of analysis and breadth in the answer. In particular, both microeconomic and macroeconomic effects must be considered. It is also necessary to relate the analysis to the context of the question, i.e. Italy's national debt as a proportion of GDP.
>
> Given that 'evaluate' is the command word, the points considered should be evaluated and there should be a concluding paragraph containing an 'informed judgement'.

Student answer

(a) A recession is usually defined as a period of two consecutive quarters of negative economic growth. From Figure 1 it can be seen that Italy was in recession in the last two quarters of 2018. Italy was also in recession during the whole of 2012.

The following diagram shows that the Italian economy is operating below full capacity following a fall in aggregate demand. The original equilibrium was Y_1. After the fall in aggregate demand, the new equilibrium is Y_2.

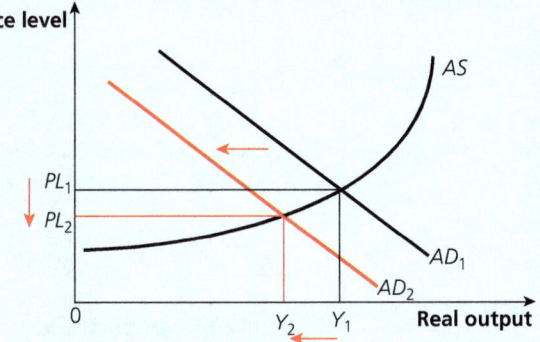

> (a) This is a good approach to answering this question: recession is defined accurately and there is relevant application from the data. A diagram is included to illustrate a recession.
> **5/5 marks awarded**

(b) In Figure 2, productivity is measured as output per worker. It can be seen that Italy's productivity is lower than that of the other countries in the chart. ⓐ

One reason is that Italy's economy is heavily regulated. This may reduce productivity if, for example, the labour market is inflexible and employers are unable to introduce more flexible working conditions. ⓑ

Another reason is that Italy has to pay large interest payments on its national debt which means that the government has limited funds available to spend on improvements to its infrastructure. Poor infrastructure, e.g. roads, internet and energy may reduce Italy's productivity. However, this may not be a major issue if the private sector invests to improve infrastructure or if there is investment from the EU. ⓒ

> (b) ⓐ It is good practice to begin with a definition of a term to be employed in the analysis. There is vague reference to the data but to secure both application marks specific use of the data should be made. ⓑ, ⓒ Two reasons are identified and explained and there is some evaluation at the end of the second point.
> **6/8 marks awarded**

Theme 4 A global perspective 87

(c) Businesses in Italy face much higher social security contributions than the average for OECD countries. These represent higher costs for Italian firms. Since these social security contributions are based on each employee they will affect both the average costs (*AC*) and marginal costs (*MC*).

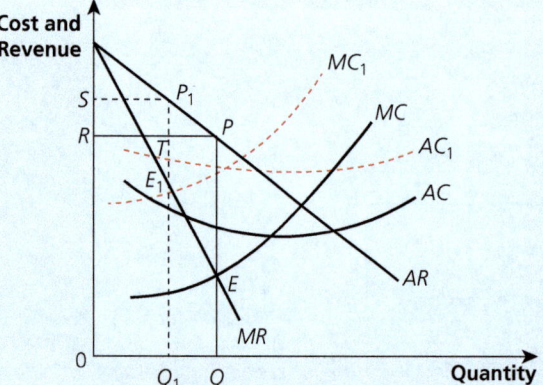

In the diagram *AC* and *MC* represent a business in an OECD country and AC_1 and MC_1 represent an Italian business. It can be seen that price would be higher (*0S*) and output lower ($0Q_1$) in Italy. In other words, its goods and services would be less competitive than American goods and services. Consequently, this might have a negative effect on Italy's trade balance with OECD countries. ⓐ However, other influencing factors may be much more significant. For example, it is implied in Extract A that membership of the euro is the main reason for Italy's poor economic performance and that if it had its own currency and devalued, its competitiveness would increase significantly. ⓑ

It can be seen from the diagram that the supernormal profit made by an Italian firm will be lower than that of a typical firm in an OECD country. This may mean that Italian firms have fewer funds to invest in new capital equipment with the result that they are likely to be less productive than firms in the USA. However, even if firms in the OECD can retain more profit, this does not necessarily mean than they will use these funds for investment. Much will depend on the state of the economy and business confidence. ⓒ

(d) Emigration refers to the exit of citizens from one country to live in another country. Figure 3 shows that the highest numbers emigrating are from the 18–39 age group while the lowest number are from the under-17 and over-65 age groups. In other words, most of the emigrants are those from the working-age group. ⓐ

> **(c)** ⓐ There is relevant analysis supported by an appropriate diagram. ⓑ There is valid evaluation of this point. ⓒ A further effect is considered with some evaluation. Overall, this is a sound answer with accurate analysis related to the context provided, combined with relevant evaluation.
> **12/12 marks awarded**

> **(d)** ⓐ The answer starts by referring directly to the context and using relevant data.

A key effect of the emigration is that the country's productive capacity would be reduced. This would result in an inward shift in the production possibility frontier and a leftward shift in the *LRAS* curve.

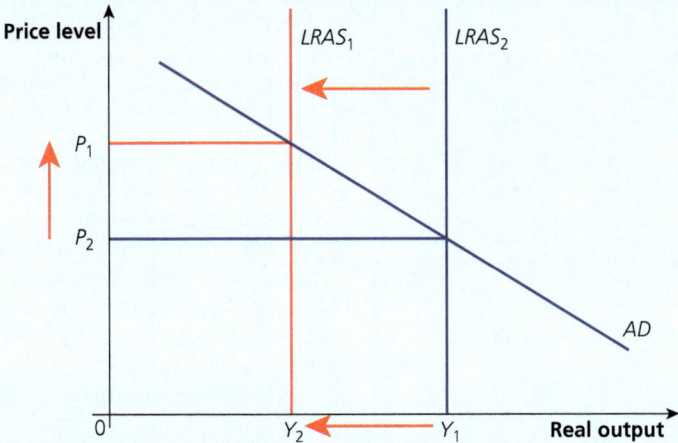

As shown in the diagram, real output would fall from Y_1 to Y_2 resulting in a decline in living standards. Italy also has a very low birth rate so the problem of emigration will result in a significant fall in the size of the country's working population. However, it is possible that immigration into Italy could offset the fall in working population caused by emigration although many of the people arriving from north Africa may not be eligible to stay in Italy. b

b The diagram is accurate and illustrates clearly the impact of emigration on real output. It is supported by an accurate explanation and concludes with some evaluation.

Emigration by people in the 18–39 age group may be particularly significant because workers in this age group are often thought to be the most productive and adaptable. This could result in a fall in productivity and, consequently, a fall in the rate of economic growth. On the other hand, unemployment in Italy is very high so the emigrants might be better off by moving abroad to find employment. Further, they could boost the Italian economy by sending remittances back to their families in Italy. Remittances are funds that emigrants earn abroad and send back to their home countries mainly to support the families that they have left behind. These would not only help to increase the living standards of those families but also improve the country's current account on the balance of payments since remittances are part of 'current transfers'. c

c Again good use is made of the data to analyse the possible impact of emigration on the Italian economy. There is some good evaluation of the possible effect of remittances on the current account.

If those emigrating from Italy are the best-educated workers, then this represents a brain drain. This could further depress economic growth in Italy because these workers are likely to be the most productive. However, the extract indicates that fewer than one in three 25–34-year-olds has a university degree.

Questions & Answers

Also, even if these are the most educated workers, they might return to Italy if economic conditions improve, so the problems might only be short term. d

Emigration has contributed to a fall in Italy's population since 2014 from 60.8 million to 60.5 million in 2018. This could have some benefits for particular markets. For example, it might mean a lower demand for houses in the future so causing average house prices to fall. It could also mean that demand for private education and healthcare would fall causing a fall in the revenues and profits of those companies providing them. The state might need to spend less money on healthcare and education facilities so that tax revenues could be used for other services. However, if life expectancy is increasing then the demand for houses might still increase as there may be more single-person households. Similarly, if there is an ageing population there is likely to be more demand for healthcare and social care. e

d There is a brief consideration of the possibility of a brain drain with evaluation.

e This paragraph considers possible effects on the public finances and includes some microeconomic analysis which is evaluated.

Despite some good analysis, there are some weaknesses. In particular, consideration of microeconomic implications is limited and there is no concluding paragraph containing an informed judgement/conclusion. Level 3 for knowledge, application and analysis and Level 2 for evaluation.
16/25 marks awarded

Student answer

(e) National debt refers to the cumulative total of past government borrowing. One way by which Italy's national debt as a proportion of GDP could be decreased is by an increase in taxation. If income tax is increased then aggregate demand would be reduced. As a result of higher income taxes disposable income will be reduced. Therefore, consumer spending will fall. Since consumption is a component of aggregate demand (*AD*), this will lead to a leftward shift in the *AD* curve. In turn this will lead to a decrease in real output which could cause an increase in unemployment. However, if other components of *AD* increase, e.g. government expenditure, investment or net trade, then *AD* may not fall. a

At a microeconomic level higher income tax rates may reduce the incentive for individuals to work or to do overtime. This could result in an increase in costs for firms because they may have to increase overtime payments employ more staff. This could mean that firms have to raise prices which could reduce the competitiveness of their goods. b

Another economic effect of an increase in taxation would be a fall in the fiscal deficit. As the level of tax rises then the gap between government expenditure and tax revenues would decrease. Eventually, tax revenues might exceed government expenditure so that there would be a fiscal surplus. This could then be used to reduce the national debt. However, in the short term government expenditure on automatic stabilisers, e.g. welfare benefits, might increase if the higher taxes cause a reduction in aggregate demand and a higher unemployment rate. c

(e) a, b These paragraphs get straight to the heart of the question by considering a macroeconomic and a microeconomic effect of tax increases as a means of reducing the national debt. There is brief evaluation of the first point.

c This paragraph might have been better used to begin the answer but it provides analysis and evaluation of the impact on the fiscal deficit.

90 **Pearson Edexcel A-level Economics A**

An increase in taxation on incomes could also cause a fall in the rate of inflation. This is because if consumers have less disposable income then there will be less demand for goods and services. This could cause a leftward shift in aggregate demand which would result a fall in the price level. However, if there was an increase in indirect taxes such as VAT then there could be a rise in prices which might trigger an increase in wage demands resulting in a wage–price spiral. d

An alternative method of reducing the national debt would be to cut public expenditure. Since public expenditure (G) is a component of AD and an injection into the circular flow, there would be a downward multiplier effect on GDP. Diagrammatically, the leftward shift in the AD curve would result in a fall in the price level and in real output. However, with a fall in real output, national debt as a proportion of GDP may not decrease. At a microeconomic level, cuts in public expenditure might affect particular sectors and firms in the economy. For example, if healthcare spending was cut and this caused a fall in demand for pharmaceuticals, this in turn would lead to a reduction in revenues and profits for these companies. e

Some economists argue that raising taxes and reducing government expenditure would cause GDP to fall and would, therefore, be unsuccessful in reducing the national debt as a proportion of GDP. Instead, they suggest that it would be more appropriate to adopt reflationary policies in order to increase GDP by cutting taxes and raising public expenditure. The higher GDP might mean that the national debt falls as a proportion of GDP. Further, a higher GDP would lead to a reduction in unemployment, higher consumer spending and enable businesses to make higher profits, all of which should lead to an increase in tax revenues f

Reflationary policy is regarded as a high-risk strategy because the financial markets might fear that Italy would default on its debts, causing a rise in interest rates on government bonds. The danger of raising taxes is that it could cause the country to go into recession with the result that the national debt as a proportion of GDP would increase. Therefore, the least undesirable policy may be to cut public expenditure because this would provide more space for the private sector to grow. In the case of the UK, austerity measures — mainly reductions in public expenditure — have not caused unemployment. Indeed, by 2019, unemployment is at a 40-year low and the employment rate has never been higher. g

d The impact on the price level is considered and evaluated.

e There is relevant consideration of the macroeconomic and microeconomic effects of cutting public expenditure.

f Here there is a contrasting view of how the national debt might be reduced indicating that the student understands different perspectives.

g This final paragraph provides a synthesis of the material covered and provides an informed judgement — a necessary requirement for a Level 3 evaluation mark. The analysis is sound but at least one diagram should have been included in a question of this nature. Low Level 4 for knowledge, application and analysis.
21/25 marks awarded

Questions & Answers

Question 2 Robots and the economy

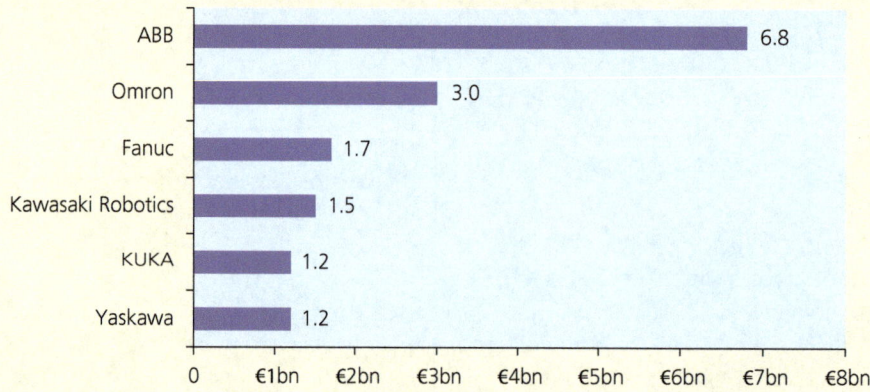

Figure 1 Largest companies in the global industrial robot market in 2017, based on revenue from industrial robot sales in € billion. The total revenue of companies manufacturing industrial robots was about €40 billion in 2017

Source: www.statista.com/statistics/257177/global-industrial-robot-market-share-by-company/

Figure 2 Percentage share of jobs with the highest and lowest risk of automation in England
Source: www.statista.com/chart/17491/jobs-at-risk-from-automation-in-england/

Extract A Robots and jobs

A variety of new technologies including advanced robotics and better, faster computers threaten the jobs of millions of people worldwide. A 2013 paper by Oxford University academics Carl Frey and Michael Osborne warned that around 47% of jobs in the USA were at high risk of being automated. However, according to analysis by the OECD in 2018, these fears are somewhat exaggerated. The researchers found that only 14% of jobs in OECD countries — which include the USA, UK, Canada and Japan — are 'highly automatable', meaning their probability of automation is 70% or higher. This forecast is much less pessimistic than the 2013 study, but it is still significant, implying that around 66 million jobs could be lost.

The reason that the OECD's estimate of job losses is lower than the Oxford research is that only some parts of a person's job may be automated. For example, in the case of a machine operator, that part involved in operating the machine could be automated but other responsibilities such as overseeing the work of juniors could not.

Although the OECD report is less pessimistic about job losses, it suggests that the impact of this new technology will still be felt by groups already under threat in today's labour markets: low-skilled workers and the young. The reason is that almost 20% of people aged 20 and below in OECD countries work in low-skilled jobs, like cleaning and food preparation, while 34% are in sales and personal services. All these are jobs that may disappear with automation.

The OECD report suggests that technology will also bring new jobs. However, governments will need to provide education and training for those whose jobs are most at risk.

Adapted from: www.theverge.com/2018/4/3/17192002/ai-job-loss-predictions-forecasts-automation-oecd-report

Extract B Robots and government policy

The increasing use of robots will cause economic dislocation and a growing sense of inequality. The argument is that everything we need will soon be produced so cheaply, that we can all have lots of it — if only the current owners don't keep all the profits for themselves. Some left-wing thinkers are much gloomier — worrying that these trends will lead to a significant increase in poverty and inequality as workers are made redundant. A possible solution is to provide a universal basic income. This means everybody gets a basic wage, whether they are working or not.

Another policy suggested by Bill Gates is that a tax should be placed on the use of robots. In essence, a legal personality should be given to robots leading to the emergence of an electronic ability to pay, which should be recognised for tax purposes. Consequently, a specific tax personality would have to be granted to robots. Taxing robots raises issues that go beyond national borders and will need to be analysed globally.

Adapted from: www.oecd.org/forum/oecdyearbook/how-taxing-robots-could-help-bridge-future-revenue-gaps.htm

Questions & Answers

(a) With reference to Figure 1, calculate the four-firm concentration ratio for the global industrial robot market. (5 marks)

> It is a good idea to show the calculations because even if the final calculation is incorrect, marks may be secured for the method used.

(b) With reference to Figure 1 and your own knowledge, discuss the significance of the concentration ratio for economic efficiency. (12 marks)

> It is a good idea to explain the term 'economic efficiency' with reference to allocative, productive and dynamic efficiency. Again, evaluation is required because the command word is 'discuss'.

(c) With reference to Figure 2, examine why the jobs of waiters/waitresses are more at risk than those of medical practitioners. (8 marks)

> Focus on two reasons with some linked explanation of each and specific reference to the data in Figure 2.
>
> Finally, evaluation is required because the command word is 'examine'.

EITHER

(d) With reference to the information provided and your own knowledge, evaluate the microeconomic and macroeconomic effects of an increase in the use of robots in an economy. (25 marks)

> It is important to ensure there is both depth of analysis and breadth in the answer. In particular, both microeconomic and macroeconomic effects must be considered. It is also necessary to relate the analysis to the context of the question, i.e. the impact of the increased use of robots in the economy.
>
> Given that 'evaluate' is the command word, the points considered should be evaluated and there should be a concluding paragraph containing an 'informed judgement'.

OR

(e) Evaluate the likely microeconomic and macroeconomic impact of the introduction of universal basic income. (25 marks)

> As with (d), it is important to ensure there is both depth of analysis and breadth in the answer. In particular, both microeconomic and macroeconomic effects must be considered. It is also necessary to relate the analysis to the context of the question, i.e. the introduction of universal basic income.
>
> Given that 'evaluate' is the command word, the points considered should be evaluated and there should be a concluding paragraph containing an 'informed judgement'.

Paper 3, Section C

Student answer

(a) The four-firm concentration ratio is the proportion if the market is supplied by the largest four firms in the market. In this case it would be:

€6.8bn + €3.0bn + €1.7bn + €1.5bn = €13bn

€13bn ÷ €40bn × 100 = 32.5%

(b) There are two main types of efficiency: allocative efficiency — the output at which price = marginal cost (MC); and productive efficiency — output at the lowest point on the average cost (AC) curve. ⓐ

A low concentration ratio would imply that the market is very competitive with no firms having a significant share of the market. In a perfectly competitive market in the long run there would be both allocative efficiency and productive efficiency. This is illustrated in the diagram which shows that at output q^* price is equal to MC and output is at the lowest point on the AC curve. ⓑ

(a) This is a good approach to answering this question: the steps in the calculation are shown and the correct answer is given.
5/5 marks awarded

(b) ⓐ The identification and accurate definition of two types of efficiency is a useful way to begin an answer to a question of this nature. ⓑ, ⓒ There is valid analysis of the significance of low concentration ratio and a high concentration ratio supported by relevant diagrams.

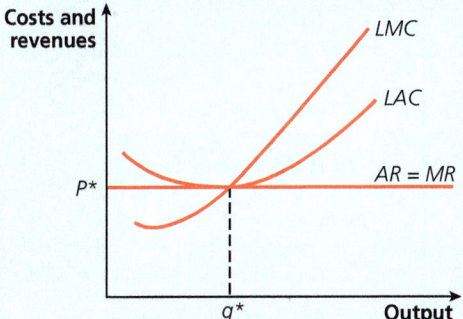

In contrast, a high concentration ratio in an industry would imply that a firm or firms supply a large proportion of the market. This might enable them to collude and behave like a monopolist. In the following diagram it can be seen that a profit-maximising monopolist is neither allocatively efficient (because price is higher than marginal cost) nor productively efficient because output is less than the lowest point on the AC curve. ⓒ

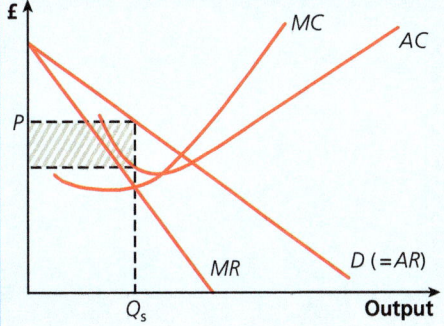

Theme 4 A global perspective   95

Questions & Answers

However, the above analysis of monopoly ignores the fact that it might be benefiting from economies of scale and is producing at lower *AC* than a firm under perfect competition. Further, the analysis relates to static efficiency, i.e. at a point in time with a given state of technology. In the long run firms might be dynamically efficient benefiting from improvements in efficiency resulting from new technology which would reduce average costs. **d**

(c) In Figure 2, waiters and waitresses have a very high risk (72.81%) of losing jobs as a result of automation whereas the risk to medical practitioners (doctors) is only 18.11%. **a**

One reason why waiters and waitresses are at a high risk of losing their jobs as a result of automation is because technology is already available to replace the tasks they perform. For example, the whole process from taking orders for food to its provision to the customer could be carried out by a robot or other forms of technology. However, where there is a demand for personal service, the replacement of people by robots is less likely. **b**

In contrast, many of the tasks performed by doctors cannot easily be performed by a robot, e.g. diagnosis of complex illnesses; the need to talk through all the possible symptoms and to evaluate their significance. However, robotic surgery is already being used in some operations although a consultant may still need to oversee the process. **c**

(d) An increase in the use of robots in an economy is likely to be very disruptive. It is estimated by the OECD that 14% of jobs in OECD countries are at risk from the use of robots. If there is no alternative work then there will be a significant increase in unemployment in these countries. **a**

This increase in unemployment would impose a considerable financial burden on the public finances of these countries in terms of lower tax revenues and increased welfare payments. Faced with such a deterioration in public finances governments might be forced to increase taxes or reduce public expenditure in other areas. However, some economists argue that this new technology will lead to an increase in productivity and to a higher rate of economic growth. In other words it should lead to a rightward shift in the *LRAS* which would cause a fall in the price level and an increase in real output. In turn higher real output should lead to higher real incomes and to increased consumer spending. It is possible that this will lead to the creation of new jobs and/or to an expansion in employment in existing occupations. For example, the number of hairdressers has increased by 50% since 2010 while more pet owners are demanding the services of pet psychologists. **b**

d The last paragraph includes some relevant evaluation of the issues. Unfortunately this is a generic answer with no reference to Figure 1. Therefore it could not secure a Level 3 mark for knowledge, application and analysis.
8/12 marks awarded

(c) **a** There is precise reference to the data which is necessary to secure application marks. **b, c** Two reasons are identified and explained and there is some evaluation of each point.
7/8 marks awarded

(d) **a** An introductory paragraph that makes use of the information provided.

b There is relevant analysis using relevant macroeconomic concepts and it includes evaluation. However, it could have been enhanced with an *AD/AS* diagram.

From Figure 2 it is clear that some workers are at greater risk of losing their jobs than others. For example, shelf fillers, bar staff and farm workers appear to be at much greater risk of losing their jobs than teachers or dentists. Therefore, those most likely to be made redundant are the low-skilled and younger workers. In the extract it states that 'almost 20% of people aged 20 and below in OECD countries work in low-skilled jobs, like cleaning and food preparation, while 34% are in sales and personal services' — jobs that might well disappear. As demand for labour falls in occupations such as farming, the wage rate would also fall relative to other occupations that are less affected. This could result in an increase in inequality with the Gini coefficient increasing. However, much will depend on the extent to which the incomes gained from those with high-tech skills and the owners of these industries are redistributed to those made redundant. In turn, this would depend on the extent to which governments use taxes and government expenditure to redistribute incomes. Also, governments might adopt the suggestion of Bill Gates of imposing a tax on robots, the revenue from which could be used for redistribution. c

The impact of new robotic technology could be limited in the short run at least because of a variety of factors. First, they may prove to be very expensive making the switch from human workers to robots less attractive. Secondly, pressure groups such as trade unions and politicians may block the introduction of this new technology. Further, there may be resistance to the use of this technology by consumers, e.g. in social care or in driverless cars or on railways. d

(e) Universal basic income (UBI) is designed to provide an income for all citizens whether they are working or not. It has been trialled in several countries including Finland and some areas of the USA. a

One aim of UBI is to ensure that no citizens should have to live in absolute poverty (where they are unable to afford the basic necessities of life such as food and shelter). It should also help to reduce inequality because everyone in the country would receive a certain level of income. Under the systems that operate in many countries, if people are not entitled to state benefits then they may be destitute. UBI should overcome this problem. However, a key problem with UBI is that it would cost a considerable amount of money to implement, especially if it is to be at a level to eliminate absolute poverty and reduce the numbers living in relative poverty. b

---

c There is relevant microeconomic analysis related to the impact on particular occupations. Again, a diagram could have been included to illustrate the impact on the wage rate in one of the occupations mentioned. The issue of inequality is also identified and evaluated. d The final paragraph contains evaluation but an 'informed judgement' is missing from this answer. This would limit the answer to a Level 2 mark for evaluation. The knowledge, application and analysis would score Level 3.

18/25 marks awarded

(e) a An introductory paragraph that provides a basic explanation of UBI and use of own knowledge to give examples of where it has been implemented. b There is relevant macroeconomic analysis and evaluation of the possible impact on inequality and poverty. However, more explanation and chains of reasoning are required, e.g. use of concepts such as Lorenz curves and Gini coefficients.

Questions & Answers

UBI could result in a decrease in incentives to work because people will receive an income without having to work. This could lead to a fall in the employment rate and to an increase in the inactivity rate. Further, to finance UBI, the government would almost certainly have to increase taxes. In turn both UBI and higher taxes could create disincentives to work if disposable income is reduced. Consequently there could be a fall in the rate of economic growth which could lead to a fall in tax revenues. This could result in a deterioration in the public finances with ever-increasing fiscal deficits and to an increasing national debt. At a microeconomic level, UBI could cause shortages of labour for particular occupations, especially those that are perceived to be low status, dangerous or poorly paid. Firms in such occupations may be forced to increase wages to attract more workers which would increase their costs. This could lead to higher prices or to a fall in profits. **c**

It is argued by some economists that UBI is desirable because the individual would be free to pursue creative, entrepreneurial or humanitarian causes. In turn this could lead to an increase in productivity as well as to an increase in national happiness or national wellbeing, which some economists think should be given higher priority than economic growth. Some research suggests that national happiness increases with income up to a certain level of income but then the correlation is weak so national happiness would not increase for all citizens. Also of significance is the degree of inequality within the country: high inequality is often associated with less happiness so UBI might contribute to an increase in national happiness. **d**

Overall, the impact of UBI on a country will depend on the level at which it is set and the extent to which it can be financed without causing too much strain on the public finances. One reason for introducing UBI is that many jobs will be replaced by robots and if this raises productivity significantly then the subsequent increase in economic growth will see a large rise in tax revenues so enabling a government to fund such a scheme. At present it is not possible to determine whether UBI is a viable proposition for most countries. **e**

c There is analysis relating to the impact on incentives to work although the use of concepts such as the Laffer curve (with diagram) could have enhanced the discussion of the effect of tax rises on incentives to work and tax revenues. There is also relevant microeconomic analysis related to the impact on particular businesses. Again, a diagram could have been included to illustrate the impact on the wage rate in one of the occupations mentioned. It would have been useful to include some evaluation in this paragraph.

d This paragraph considers the impact of UBI on economic growth and on national happiness, a Theme 2 concept. It is important to remember that Paper 3 is synoptic so analysis should be drawn from topics covered in the entire syllabus. **e** The final paragraph attempts to provide an 'informed judgement' with the final sentence indicating the high degree of uncertainty associated with providing a definitive conclusion to such a question. Despite this, the rest of the evaluation is rather limited so the answer would score a Level 2 mark for evaluation. Given the deficiencies in the knowledge, application and analysis the answer would score a Level 3.

16/25 marks awarded

Knowledge check answers

1. An increase in protectionist policies; a significant rise in transport costs.
2. Loss of low-skilled jobs to countries with low wages causing a downward pressure on wages or leading to an increase in unemployment; more demand for workers with higher skills causing a rise in their incomes.
3. Free trade should result in more choice. It should result in lower prices and, therefore, an increase in consumer surplus.
4. An increase in export prices; a decrease in import prices; an appreciation in the exchange rate of a country's currency.
5. Free trade between member countries.
6. Tariffs distort comparative advantage. Consequently resources will not be allocated efficiently with the result that global output and living standards will fall.
7. Various factors could be responsible, including: relatively high unit labour costs; relatively low productivity; a high inflation rate relative to other countries; overvaluation of the currency; non-price factors including poor design, poor quality and unreliability of the product.
8. Expenditure-switching policies relate to policies designed to change the composition of expenditure between domestic and foreign goods, e.g. tariffs, whereas expenditure-reducing policies are designed to reduce aggregate demand, e.g. contractionary fiscal policy.
9. This could result in a loss of confidence in the bolivar (the Venezuelan currency), so causing its value to fall. People would sell bolivars and buy other currencies such as the US dollar on the foreign exchange market so causing a depreciation in the value of the bolivar relative to the US$.
10. The current account would deteriorate, i.e. the deficit would get larger, since the Marshall–Lerner condition had not been fulfilled.
11. That country's international competitiveness would decline, since a relatively lower productivity rate implies that its unit costs of production would rise relative to its competitors.
12. No, because relative poverty measures the proportion of people below a set level, e.g. 60% of the median income. Consequently, there will always be a proportion of the population living in relative poverty unless there was a command economy in which everyone received the same income.
13. The Lorenz curve would move further away from the 45° line.
14. The demand for and supply of many commodities tends to be price inelastic. Consequently a shift in either the demand curve or the supply curve would cause a significant change in the price.
15. The Harrod–Domar model ignores the importance of human capital. Also, the savings gap may be filled in other ways, e.g. aid; FDI.
16. It will increase because there will be more dependants, i.e. those under 16 and over 65, relative to the number of workers.
17. If individuals have no property rights, they will not have any collateral to secure a loan from a bank to start a business.
18. Trade liberalisation might make it very difficult for developing countries to develop their manufacturing industries because they would be unable to compete with established industries in developed economies that are benefiting from economies of scale.
19. Market-orientated strategies include trade liberalisation and removal of government subsidies. Interventionist strategies include managed exchange rates and development of human capital.
20. The foreign currency earned from tourism may be used to buy capital goods and raw materials needed for infrastructure and new manufacturing industries.
21. FDI is undertaken by transnational companies with the aim of making a profit for shareholders, whereas aid refers to grants or loans at less than the market rate of interest (called concessional loans) given to developing countries by governments, international organisations or non-governmental organisations.
22. This refers to the interest paid on loans. In the case of a government, it means that it would have less money available to spend on public services.
23. There is a danger that countries whose debts have been cancelled will follow policies that result in further debts being built up in the future.
24. These countries faced very large budget deficits and increasing national debts and found it very difficult to finance these. Consequently they were forced to seek loans from the IMF. Strict conditions were attached to these loans, for example, austerity measures to reduce fiscal deficits.
25. A bank failure could cause problems for consumers and businesses which are not customers of the bank. For example, firms (which do not have accounts at the bank) may face a loss of trade because customers of the bank may have lost all their deposits.
26. Welfare expenditure is expected to be about 27% of total managed expenditure in 2019–20.
27. When the income tax rate rises people will be less willing to work in favour of more leisure. This is because the loss of earnings from work is now lower, i.e. the opportunity cost of work is lower. (This is called the substitution effect.)

Knowledge check answers

28 Income tax is a progressive tax. Therefore, an increase in income tax rates would make income distribution more even.

29 It is likely that public finances would deteriorate: automatic stabilisers mean that government expenditure on social benefits for the unemployed would increase, while tax revenues would fall (not only from incomes but also from a reduction in revenues from expenditure taxes, e.g. VAT, and from corporation tax).

30 Banks may be unwilling to lend if they consider the risks of non-repayment to be too great. A lack of confidence might mean that firms and consumers are unwilling to borrow.

Index

Note: Bold pages numbers refer to definitions.

A
absolute advantage **8**
absolute poverty 28, **29**
access to credit and banking 38
aid 47–48
appreciation of currency 19, 21
automatic stabilisers **61**

B
balance of payments
  capital and financial account 16
  components 16–17
  current account 12, 14, 16–18, 20
banking industry, regulation 53
banks
  central bank role 53
  traditional role 52
bilateral aid 47
bilateral trade agreements 10–11, 25, 64
buffer stock schemes 44

C
capital expenditure 55
capital and financial account 16
capital flight 31, 37–38
capital gains tax 58
capitalism, and inequality 31
central banks, role 53
China, opening up to world trade 7
civil wars 39
commodity markets, volatility 36
common currency 13
common markets 12
communication cost decline 7
community-based development 50
companies, benefit of trade liberalisation 41
comparative advantage **9**
  changes in 10
  distortion of 13, 43
  limitations 10
  underlying assumptions 9
competitive devaluations/depreciations 21
competitiveness *see* international competitiveness
concentration ratio 94, **95**
consumers 8, 15, 41
corporation tax 58
corruption 39
country's economy 7–8, 41
country's terms of trade 11–12
credit, provision of 52
credit and banking, access to 38
crowding out 57, **62**
currency
  devaluation and depreciation 20
  revaluation and appreciation 19
  exchange rates *see* exchange rates
currency fluctuations, elimination (monetary unions) 13
currency markets, government intervention in 21
currency wars **21**
current account 12
  components 16
  correction 14
  exchange rate change effects 22
  UK 17–18
current account deficits 16–18
current account surpluses 17, 18
current expenditure 55
current transfers 16
custom unions 12
customs duties 14–15
'cyclical' fiscal deficit 61

D
debt interest 56, 62
debt relief 48
  arguments for/against debt cancellation 48–49
deglobalisation 8
demand—supply curve, and price inelasticity of commodities 36
demographic factors, impact on growth and development 38

depreciation of a currency 20, 21, 23, 25
deregulation 25
devaluation of a currency 20
devaluation/depreciation
  competitive 21
  of the country's currency 18, 22, 64
developing economies *see* emerging and developing economies
development, measures of 33
direct controls 63
direct tax rates, economic effect of changes in 58–60
direct taxes, versus indirect taxes 58
discretionary fiscal policy 56, 61, 62
dumping prevention 14
Dutch disease 35

E
East African Common Market 12
economic change, impact on development of inequality 31
economic development 69, 75, 78
economic growth 75, 77
  and depreciation 23
education and skills, impact on growth and development 39
education and training schemes 25
effective exchange rates 19
emerging and developing economies 33–50
  factors influencing growth and development 34–39
  'resource curse' 12
  share in world exports 10, 11
  strategies influencing growth and development 39–50
emigration 86, 88–90
employment 23, 41
  and change in income tax rates 59
  and change in indirect taxes 60
employment protection 14
environment, impact of globalisation on 8

Theme 4 A global perspective 101

Index

equality
  impact of protectionist policies on 16
  and level of public expenditure 57
equities 52
exchange rate policy 63
exchange rate systems 19
exchange rates 19–25, 70
  changes 11, 12
  depreciation/devaluation 18, 19, 21, 23
  effects of changes 22–23
  government intervention 21
  managed 43
  revaluation/appreciation 18
excise duties 58
expenditure-reducing policies 18
expenditure-switching policies 18
export earnings, fluctuations 34
export increase, through trade liberalisation 41
external costs of globalisation 8
external shocks to the global economy 64–65, 66
externalities **52**

F

fair trade schemes 46, 47–48
financial crowding out 57
financial markets, role in the economy 52
financial sector 52, 71
  central bank role 53
  market failure 52–53
fiscal (budget) deficits 61, 62, 63
  significance of the size of 72–73
fiscal policy 61, 63
fiscal surpluses 62
fixed exchange rates 19
floating exchange rates 20, 42
foreign currency transactions 21, 52
foreign direct investment (FDI) **6**, 7, 13, 16, 42
  and depreciation 23
  and higher income tax rates 60
  and higher indirect tax rates 60
  promotion of 41
foreign exchange gap 37
forward markets for currencies and commodities 52
free market economy 31
free trade 7–8, 10, 13
  restrictions on 14–16
free trade areas 12

G

Gambian economy 73–78
GDP 25, 37, 38, 45
  and IMF quotas from countries 50
  and level of aid 47
  and level of public expenditure 56–57, 62
  and UK balance of payments on current account 17
  world, and world trade 6, 7
geriatric industries, protection 14
Gini coefficient 29, 30, 73, 75, 76
global competitiveness index 23–24
global financial crisis 8, 52, 62
global trade imbalances, significance 18–19
global warming 8
globalisation 6–8
governments
  central banks as banker to 53
  impact of globalisation on 8
  impact of protectionist policies on 16
  and their ability to control global companies 65
growth and development
  factors influencing 34–39
  strategies influencing 39–50

H

Harrod–Domar model 37
human capital 25, 42
human development index (HDI) 33, 69

I

import restrictions 14
import substitution 43
income balance 16
income distribution
  and changes in income tax 59
  and changes in indirect taxes 60
income inequality 29–31
income redistribution 56
income tax 58
income tax rates, effect of increase in 58–60
independent monetary policy, loss of 13
indirect tax rates, economic effect of changes in 60–61
indirect taxes, versus direct taxes 58
industrialisation: the Lewis model 45–46
inequality 29–31, 71–72
  and globalisation 8
  impact of economic change and development on 31
  income and wealth inequality 29–31
  measures to reduce 63
  significance of capitalism 31
inequality-adjusted HDI (IHDI) 33
infant industries, protection 14
inflation, danger of 62–63
inflation rate 12
  following depreciation 23
  relative 11, 20
infrastructure
  government expenditure on 25
  and growth and development 38, 43
interest rates
  changes in 63
  relative 20
international competitiveness 18, 22, 23–25
  benefits/problems of 25
  boosting through supply-side policies 18, 25, 64

Index

factors influencing 24–25
measures 23–24
measures to increase 64
price and non-price factors 23
international economics 6–27
international institutions 49–50
International Monetary Fund (IMF) 49–50
interventionist policies 18
interventionist strategies influencing growth and development 40, 42–44
investment incentives 25
inward-looking strategies 43
Italy's economy 84–91

J
J-curve effect 22
joint ventures 43

L
labour market flexibility 25
lack of competition 43
Laffer curve 58, 59
law of comparative advantage 7
law of diminishing returns **45**
Lewis model 44–45
living standards 12
impact of protectionist policies 16
and public expenditure 57
Lorenz curve 29–30, 75, 76
low income elasticity of demand for primary products 35

M
macroeconomic policies in a global context 63
controlling transnational companies 65
fiscal and other policy use 63–64
problems facing policymakers when applying policies 65–66
response to external shocks 64–65
macroeconomy, state role in 55–66

managed exchange rates 19, 43
market-based policies 18
market bubbles 53
market failure in the financial sector 52–53
market-oriented strategies influencing growth and development 40–42
market rigging 53
Marshall–Lerner condition 22
Mercosur 12
microfinance schemes 38, 42
modern monetary theory (MMT) 64
monetary policy 53, 63–64
monetary unions 13
money supply, changes in 63–64
money transfers 52
moral hazard 52
multi-dimensional poverty index (MPI) 33
multilateral aid 47

N
national debt 61
factors influencing size of 62
Italy 87, 90–91
measures to reduce 63
significance of the size of 62–63
The Gambia 75, 76
natural disasters 35, 62
nominal exchange rate 19
non-economic factors affecting growth and development 39
non-government organisations (NGOs) 50
non-tariff barriers 15
non-wage costs 24

O
oil price increase 79–80
opportunity costs 9, 62

P
patterns of trade 10–1
political priorities 56
political stability/instability 20, 39

poor governance 39
population growth 38
population size and age distribution 56, 62
poverty and inequality 28–32
absolute 28, 29
measures to reduce 63
relative 28, 29, 56
poverty line 28
Prebisch–Singer hypothesis 12, 35–36
price elasticity of demand 61
price level
and change in income tax 59
and change in indirect taxes 60
price transparency (monetary unions) 3
primary income 15
primary industries development 46
primary product dependency 12, 34–36
privatisation 25, 42
producers 8, 15
productivity and growth
Italy 86, 87
and public expenditure 56
progressive tax 57, 59
property rights, absence of 39
proportional tax 58
protectionism 43, 64
arguments supporting 14
by developed countries 35
protectionist policies 14, 18, 25
impact of 15–16
public expenditure 55–57, 62
public finance 55–57, 61–63
taxation 57–61
public sector borrowing 61–63
public sector reform 25
purchasing power parity (PPP) analysis 20

Q
quantitative easing 63–64
quantity theory of money 64
quotas 15

Index

R
raw material price changes 11
real exchange rate 19, **24**
   and competitiveness 24
real GDP 8, 62, 84
real output and employment
   and changes in indirect taxes 60
   and increase in income tax rates 59
real wages, higher 41
recession 61, 62, 86, 87
regional trade agreements 7, 10, 11
   costs and benefits 13
   possible conflict with WTO 13
regressive tax 58
relative exchange rates, changes in 11
relative export prices 23
relative inflation rate 11, 20
relative interest rates 20
relative poverty 28, 56
   causes of changes 29
   measures of 29
relative unit labour costs 23
resource crowding out 57
restrictions on free trade 14–16
revaluation of currency 19
robots and the economy 92–98

S
saving by individuals and firms 52
savings and investment levels 37
secondary income 16
social security contributions, Italy 86, 88
special drawing rights (SDR) 50
specialisation and trade 8–10
speculation 20, 53
stabilisation programmes 49
state of the economy, and exchange rates 20
state role in the macroeconomy 55–66
stock exchanges 52
'structural' fiscal deficit 61
subsidies
   effect of removal of 41
   to domestic producers 15
supply-side policies to improve competitiveness 18, 25, 64

T
tariffs 12, 14–15, 25, 58, 64
   benefits of reduction in 40–41
tax revenues
   and changes in income tax 58–59
   and changes in indirect taxes 60
   fluctuations 34
   raising through tariffs 14
taxation 57–61
taxes, direct and indirect 58–61
terms of trade **11**–12, 72
theory of comparative advantage 9–10
tied aid 47
tourism development 45, 74, 75, 78
trade
   patterns of 10–11
   and specialisation 8–10
   terms of 11–12, 72
trade balance 16
   and change in income tax 59
   and change in indirect taxes 60
trade barriers
   impact of reducing 41
   lowering of 7, 12
   reasons for 14
trade creation 13
trade diversion 13
trade liberalisation 13, 40–41
trade war 80–82
trade-weighted exchange rate 19
trading blocs 7, **10**, 11; *see also* regional trade agreements
   types of 12–13
transaction costs, elimination (monetary unions) 13
transfer payments 55
transfer pricing **8**
   regulation 65
transnational companies (TNCs) 6, 7, 45, 46
   measures to control 65
transport cost decline 7

U
UK's current account 17–18
unemployment 23
unfair competitive advantage 14
universal basic income 94, 97–98

V
value added tax (VAT) 58, 60
volatility in commodity markets 36

W
wage costs 24
wars 39, 62
wealth inequality 29, 30–31
work incentives 58, 60
workers, impact of globalisation on 8
World Bank 28, 49, 50
world trade and world GDP, growth 6, 7, 8
World Trade Organization (WTO) 7, 14, 64
   possible conflict with regional trade agreements 13
   role in trade liberalisation 13